The INDIA COLLECTIVE

What India is Really All About

The INDIA COLLECTIVE

What India is Really All About

SECOND EDITION

Karan Mehrishi

KNOWLEDGE WORLD

KW Publishers Pvt Ltd
New Delhi

ISBN 978-93-91490-22-5 Hardback
eISBN 978-93-91490-30-0 ebook

Published in India by Kalpana Shukla

KNOWLEDGE WORLD

KW Publishers Pvt Ltd
4676/21, First Floor, Ansari Road
Daryaganj, New Delhi 110002
Phone: +91 11 43528107
Marketing: kw@kwpub.in
Editorial: production@kwpub.in
Website: www.kwpub.in

Printed and Bound in India

Contents

Dedicated to

Mummy, Papa, Guddu Chacha

For bearing with my impossibilities

"All the powers in the Universe are already ours. It is we who have put our hands before our eyes and cry that it is dark."

—Swami Vivekananda

Foreword

If you haven't visited India once, chances are that you might have certain preconceived notions about the country. For an outsider, unfamiliar with the Indian way, the country is an enigma—a complex co-existence of the rich and the poor, ancient and modern.

Not without reason, the story of legendary Indian chaos prevents foreigners from exploring the country for what it is. Once you scratch the surface, will you find your answers and understand how India actually works.

Karan has written this book with a lot of passion for his home country, and I feel that this book celebrates the diversity of India well. What stands out about the book is the fact that it presents the India story undiluted and pure.

The book rightly points out that India is a juggernaut that continues to strengthen itself with new stimuli. Gandhi's quote, "the introduction of foreigners does not necessarily destroy a nation, they merge in it. A country is one nation only when such a condition obtains in it. That country must have a faculty for assimilation; India has ever been such a country," taken from his book, *Hind Swaraj*, best summarises India's core ideas of assimilation and peaceful co-existence. In a way this decodes the Indian nation for a foreigner.

Also, while everyone is aware about India's economic potential and the pace of its growth, the 'rights to responsibility' equation remains unsolved. In my experience, no country can progress without the citizens taking the onus of development on themselves. Citizen responsibility towards the nation is therefore the key. Karan has not ignored this facet and cited its criticality in nation building.

As you read on, you will find, that this book is divided into three parts, that is, the past, present and the future. Given the magnitude of India's history and the nuances involved, insights are only possible when different epochs are understood separately.

In my own interpretation, India's past provides a glimpse of the global history as it intertwines with almost all global cultures and people. The present on the other hand represents a nation's struggles to break the very shackles that bind it. The future of India, perhaps the most interesting part, is nothing short of an attempt to imagine human potential. Given the fact that India represents 1.4 billion people, anything that pertains to India is a microcosm of all humanity.

The India Collective is a must-read book especially by those who over the years adopted India as their second intellectual home. I am one of those who kept India close to their hearts. The book is extremely well written and fascinating. One of the key attributes to a great book such as this is that it flows as if friction has vanished as a physical phenomenon and reading it flows unimpededly.

When you are reading this book, read it with an open mind. I am confident that you will take away a few perspectives that will have applicability to many geo-political issues and complex human interactions.

Happy Reading!

Dr. **Nicolas Stylianides**

"Watch your Thoughts, they become your words. Watch your words, they become actions. Watch your actions, they become habits. Watch your habits, they become character. Watch your character, it becomes your destiny."

—Lao Tzu

Preface

I began writing the first edition of this book in 2012, in the month of March, when a casual drive in New Delhi sparked an idea that led to countless sleepless nights and prolonged thinking man sessions. I often drive alone as a stress buster and my location that fateful evening was somewhere near the SDA market and IIT Delhi's main entrance. My so called eureka moment was set off amidst an otherwise fast-moving traffic that was suddenly slowed down by a random crowd trying to cross the main road, one of the arteries of Delhi.

These people were almost embracing each other, came from different communities (as apparent from religious markers) and just had one common denominator: they wanted to cross the road at any cost. As one collective unit, they raised their hands in perfect harmony, trying to stop the oncoming traffic, seamlessly coordinating their collective movement, and successfully completing the task without any disdain or prejudice for each other.

As soon as the task was completed, these people broke the collective and went their separate ways. Importantly, however, while undertaking the task, none of these people bothered which background was or was not represented in that collective. What they cared in that moment was the fact that they could not have crossed the road as individuals, a realisation that sub-consciously forced them to form a collective to get the work done. Seeing these people doing a simple act without caring about each other's background made me think deeply about India and the people who live here. If not for religious and caste-based segregation, I reckon that Indians sub-consciously share a value system that seems to be omnipresent among them. As the event unfolded in front of my eyes, I wondered whether a similar level of comfort would exist among Indians in much substantial do or die situations?

I have started to believe that a random act of crossing the road is not an end, rather it is a progenitor of several social collectives that can perform several tasks, including effective nation building. This form of purpose-built social cohesion is found in several countries, such as China's Gung-Ho Movement, South Korea's Saemaul Undong (New Village Movement) and Israel's Kibbutzim Collective Farming. Historically, these movements were effectively used as tools to create wealth and well-being for the masses via purpose-built collectivization. What is often ignored, however, is the fact that an Indian brand of social cohesions and collectivization also exists. Further research revealed that India itself is no stranger to such movements, which are imbibed in the country's democratic values.

According to my research, there are several examples from India's socio-economic history spanning business, economics, politics, governance and social structures. In fact, I believe that India's history of collectivity and co-operation is the reason behind its fundamental identity as a democracy. I am now of the opinion that the most successful definition of India then must incorporate India's 'lack of a homogenous character' and describe India as a 'Global Inductor'. I think, India is a hybrid thought that continues to evolve nonchalantly and will continue to do so in the future. Therefore, India then is not just a 'certain' country inhabited by a 'certain' people but a 'collective' for several types of people, cultures, beliefs and ethnicity. I'd like to call this seemingly impossible cohabitation of thoughts, ideals and value as the 'India Collective.'

The interesting bit is that there is an underlying alpha thought doing the rounds here, and I suspect this is something that really drives India; strangely enough, we the citizens are subconsciously connected to our collective, whether we are aware of it or not. When you read further, you will see how India inducts the best thoughts into its folds even today. Surprisingly, everything is seamlessly connected in a mesh of disparate thoughts. This is precisely how India has continued to bind multiple beliefs, plethora of people, languages, sub-cultures, and ways of thinking into one whole throughout its history.

As India stands at the cusp of superpower status, the concept of the India Collective is more vital than ever. Given the magnitude of examples, case studies and possibilities, I could only do justice to the research by dividing the book into three epochs – Past, Present and Future. After all, this book is the result of three years' worth of research and 4 hours of sleep per night. Now in its second edition, you will notice that certain numbers are older and have not been revised to 2021. This is intentional as numbers are just used as tools to explain concepts; updated numbers would not have brought about newer insights.

Nevertheless, the world has changed since 2015, given the fact that the Planning Commission is now Niti Aayog, and Plan Periods and Plan Expenditures do not exist. No to mention the Covid 19 pandemic that has changed our lives permanently. Also, some of the ideas introduced by this book in its "Edition 1" have seen some light of the day (I however, suspect that the ideators never read the book!) and are under implementation as laws and national strategies. I wish that you read the book with the same kind of passion for India as I felt while writing this book. Like my fellow Indians and friends of India, I want India to succeed and rightfully take its place in the global order. I believe that the juggernaut called India will continue to roll, and its time as an idea has arrived.

Karan Mehrishi

As Indians: Who are We?

- "This is a democracy for God's sake. Why don't things change for the better?"
- "India does not have enough literacy."
- "Respect and safety of women! Is that a joke?
- "Why can't we teach a lesson to hostile neighbour countries, who continue to torment us?"
- "There are so many people here. Is anybody serious about controlling the population?"
- "India has so much poverty."
- "Ethnic violence? That happens here all the time."
- "There is so much filth and a lack of civic sense."
- "Nobody really cares in India about anything."
- "Everyone is living for themselves."
- "This nation is doomed."
- "God knows where India is heading, *Ram Bharose*."

Does this sound familiar? For us Indians, these statements are likely to haunt us even when we are completing the most mundane of tasks every day. We feel frustration, gloom and sometimes uneasiness as we watch our beloved country precariously slide towards mediocrity. This forces us to think whether we understand the situation fully. Contrarily, whether the problem itself is elusive.

All these years, we the citizens of India seem to have just pointed fingers at 'corrupt people'—never really asking who these so-called corrupt people were in the first place. As things turned out, these people were definitely not foreigners forcibly put amongst us, but perhaps those who were ostensibly chosen by us from within ourown system. Then why does it seem that whoever enters a position of authority (democratically or otherwise) in this country becomes corrupt by default, or at least perceived to be? Worryingly, corruption is at every level of our system and not only in the great corridors of power. The most important question one must therefore ask is whether the individual or the society that spawns such individuals is at fault here. Isn't it time to look within ourselves first and end the blame game? Isn't it our collective responsibility to look after our country?

Perhaps the answers that we seek will come from the realisation that we as a nation lack a soul, the central idea of being an Indian. This may sound ridiculous in the first instance for a spiritually inclined country, but given the fact that a majority of our population lives on less than $2 a day, worsened by rampant corruption and crime against women, everything becomes uncomfortably self-explanatory.

Every successful country has a soul, a core value system upon which entire socio-economic structures are built. The United States, for example, is based on the value system of success and achievement; Germany is based on the value system of discipline and order; the United Kingdom is based around the value system of its monarch and Buckingham Palace; Japan is based on the value system of selflessness and Switzerland on the value system of neutrality. These countries are proud of their central value systems and their public and financial institutions, and the general population operates with that core idea. The problem with India is that the country currently lacks a peculiar value system on which to base a standard socioeconomic structure; this is primarily because we never really understood who we are in the first place. This confused state of flux has given India multiple parallel systems leading to nothing but the resultant chaos that is dragging us down.

Referring to the past in this context, Indians have had a glorious history and has been a forerunner in several scientific and other such momentous discoveries. To get things into perspective, we mustn't forget the fact that we were the world leaders in almost everything for much of humanity's known history. We are the originators of the world's four out of seven major religions (Hinduism, Buddhism, Sikhism and Jainism), and hence one of the most dominant influencers of global thought, yet our voice has today been drowned out on global rhetoric platforms such as the United Nations Security Council. Through the Vedas and other such texts, our forefathers/foremothers gave the world the most advanced concepts of Mathematics, Physics, Astronomy, Physiology, Metallurgy, Strategy, Economics and Literature, yet we are today struggling to use Intellectual Property Rights (IPRs) of other countries.

Despite the fact that India was home to the world's first and largest organised research universities and centres of learning such as *Takshashila* and *Nalanda*, which date back to before the fifth century AD, we are today home to one of the world's most illiterate populations, who can't even understand the simple concepts of family planning and hygiene.

When genius means money, one of the world's most intellectually gifted populations is also today one of the world's poorest; contradictory?! You tell me.

As a solution, several Indian intellectuals talk about an elusive 'all-inclusive socio-economic system' that considers all stakeholders. Unfortunately, almost none could give us a roadmap to achieve it and therefore we as a country somehow miss the larger picture. Quoted on many occasions, the crux of the matter is that we are a multi-ethnic, multi-religious, multi-lingual nation, and that is not only our characteristic but also our soul. This diversity , then, is what makes us who we are. To function in accordance with this thinking, we must work together and consequently under all circumstances, our central value system must be 'cooperation,' a concept on which we must build our socio-economic structures. We were not the world leaders for thousands of years without working as a collective unit, and obviously we must do so again if we aspire to regain our leadership.

The impediment to this renaissance, however, is the fact that we the citizens of India have misused the concept of diversity for our petty community ideologies when we should have solely concentrated on nation building. Vote bank politics, community centricity and mindless notions have destroyed the core values of our country, and there seems to be no letting up. What else explains a multi-party system where every community, which has certain issues (no matter how insignificant), tries to make a political ideology while exhibiting absolute disregard towards the larger concerns of their country?

Let's face it, a multi-party political structure will never guarantee formulation of the most important policies until there is a consensus in opinion. The multi-party system, which is also prevalent in Germany, Italy, and Japan, is successful there because ultimately all-party representatives and supporters are Germans, Italians and Japanese first and everything else later; in India, however, the reverse is true, which is the root of the problem.

If the European Union (EU), which is in fact a group of separate sovereign nations (with a history of hostilities and great wars) can make a conscious and honest effort to fortify and strengthen its Union, why on earth can't the different communities of India? We can't be more disparate than Europe. We were never a group of sovereign nations in our pasts, therefore we cannot justifiably have any reservations to make a collective and honest effort towards strengthening our country and, eventually, us all. Percolation of wealth without a collective intent cannot lead to a meaningful improvement in standards of living. In all probability, our diverse country's socioeconomic structures must be based on cooperation among the citizenry, and this must be our country's central value system.

Our differences are not important, what is important is our collectiveness because that embodies the concept of India. We must find a sense of purpose in our diversity and that is only possible if we overlook our petty differences. If we think sincerely about who we are as Indians, we will see that we are inherently connected to each other. This is mainly because we are not a democracy by choice but by fundamental character. We may have different ways of looking at things, but ultimately, we are part of a network, a hybrid thought process, that must be evolved further for our own good and prosperity.

There is an example of America in the 1940s during World War II, before the country become a global superpower. This was when women of all races, religions and creeds, who had never left their homes earlier stepped out while their fathers, brothers and husbands were away at war. These courageous and nationalist women were committed to their nation and wanted to take part in rampingup America's industrial output to win the war at all costs. For these women, some of whom left their little children at day care centres, with older relatives or sometimes even unattended, America was more important than anything else they held dear— that my dear readers is collectivity, and that is how you actually build a successful nation.

"If there is one place on the face of the Earth where all the dreams of living men have found a home from the very earliest days when man began the dream of existence, it is India."

— Romain Rolland, Scholar

What India has been

"From the time of the Rig Veda till today, India has been the home of different religions and the Indian genius adopted a policy of live and let live towards them. Indian religion never quite understood the idea of exclusive worship. Indian religious tradition admits all forms in which the single truth is reflected."

—Sarvepalli Radhakrishnan,
second President of the Republic of India

Historically, most human past is concentrated around the world's water bodies. In their ground-breaking book, *The Ancient River Civilizations: Western Man and the Modern World* (first published in 1973), authors Peter A. Clayton and John Dent have discussed in detail how ancient river systems were the primary centres of the civilised man's socio-economic existence and eventual evolution. Perhaps, to an extent, *The Emergence of Civilization: From Hunting and Gathering to Agriculture, Cities and the state of the New East* by archaeologist and historian Charles Keith Maisels is another good reference.

Not without reason, just one look at the trajectory of Earth's most pivotal civilisations reveals that human socio-economic development has centred itself adjacent to our rivers, seas and oceans. Egyptian (Nile River), Mesopotamian (Tigris/Euphrates Rivers), Indus Valley (Indus River and tributaries), Mayan (Motagua River) and Huang He (Yellow River) are all ancient civilisations often termed as the progenitors of the modern man.

It is so believed that these successful civilisations started out just as several isolated and vulnerable human habitations that evolved because of their proximity to a fertile land replenished with minerals by downstream rivers and an easy access to water. As these habitations developed further, they understood the initially overlooked benefit—access to other habitations located up or down these river streams. As modern trade and commerce developed, there were apparent mutual benefits, and a symbiotic business environment was created among these former isolated habitations, eventually creating prosperous civilisations. In essence, these civilisations all started out as several habitations conjoined together to form a collective, a Civilisation. Therefore, the central thesis of their collective success was a common connection through a passing river. The river was the common thread of the people, and an association with the river (as a central sustainer) bound them together in a collectivity, giving them a sense of belonging.

In the modern world, where interconnection is the essence of globalisation, successful countries are those which have successfully integrated themselves not only with the rest of the world but within themselves first. Under all circumstances, at the centre of a successful civilisation is an idea to which every citizen has some sort of an allegiance. Nothing has changed from then until now as a common centrality has remained constant; the only difference is the way citizens associate—it was the river for the early man and it is an idea for the modern. Every society, which is successful today, has not forgotten the fact that a common idea binds all citizens together and that binding is what is today known as a country.

Civilisations have been established throughout history around central ideas, which could be rivers, common beliefs, religion or common purpose. It is pivotal to understand that if there is no central idea, there is bound to be chaos as there is lack of coherence, and hence integration is not achieved. In this context, the rivers of today are 'value systems' that bind the psyche of citizens. These value systems comprise thoughts, ideas, ideals and common goals that are shared by a certain group of people. Among them, those who believe in and imbibe these value systems form collectives and collectively build successful countries.

By applying these analogies to India as a country and Indians as a diaspora, it can be said that the nation is a value system first; a system, an economy or a religious affiliate later.

In its true sense, this book is therefore an effort towards identifying the essence of India and what it embodies. In its odyssey, the book seeks to provide answers to serious issues about our national identity and what we represent as a nation.

Thus, the book does not imagine or seek an ideal utopian society; rather, it interests itself in understanding and identifying a sustainable and progressive society that has meaningfully contributed in strengthening the Indian thought through the years. Importantly, this is done by first understanding what this society truly represents. As a matter of fact, ambiguity will be experienced on the way, but the battle is won if these ambiguities co-exist within a grand idea of our unique personality as a nation.

Formation of the Collective

The Origins

> *Matrudevo Bhava, Pitrudevo Bhava, Acharyadevo Bhava, Atithidevo Bhava*
>
> "Be one for whom; Mother is God, Father is God, Teacher is God and Guest is God"

In fifteenth-century Kashmir, Sultan Zain-ul-Abidin's concept of 'Kashmiriyat' was and still remains as the most powerful proofs of India's relentless induction of power. Even though the concept has somewhat become peripheral in light of Hindu–Muslim conflicts of interest in the valley, Kashmiriyat has survived among Kashmiris and is still associated with unity. Considered as being one of the most successful and secular Kashmiri Sultans, nothing has been more effective than his notion of bringing Kashmiris of various religions together. Without a doubt, the concept's success can be understood in the context of India as a whole. The Collective that Zain-ul-Abidin envisioned for Kashmir in order to unite his people not only gave him eminence among his varied subjects, but also provided him with strategic hold over the desperate tribes of Swat, Ladakh and Central Asia. Thus, when viewed in a broader context, Kashmiriyat serves as a microcosm of what a greater Indian nation genuinely symbolises, strategically or otherwise.

In the past, people have coined several concepts of India stemming from their philosophical belief systems. Initially this land was called Hindusthan by Central Asians, then later it was equated to the qualities of an Elephant and a Tiger. More recently, there were other concepts such as Rahul Gandhi's 'Beehive,' and Narendra Modi's 'Mother India' that have made headlines. While each of these ideologies are relevant and profound in their own right, I believe that the most successful definition of India must incorporate India's 'lack of a homogenous character' and describe India as a 'Global Inductor,' incorporating all these monikers. I think, India is a hybrid thought that continues to evolve nonchalantly and will continue doing so in the future. Therefore, India then is not just a 'certain' country inhabited by a 'certain' people, but a 'collective' for several types of people, cultures, beliefs and ethnicity; figuratively speaking, unlike a beehive there is no central queen but a central idea. I'd like to call this seemingly impossible cohabitation of thoughts, ideals and values, the 'India Collective.' Personally, my ideology is more in line with Jawahar Lal Nehru's and Atal Bihari Vajpayee's concepts of India. In his book, the *Discovery of India,* Nehru has aptly described Hinduism as continuing to evolve as a religion by assimilating several cultures throughout its history, related to what B.K. Smith suggested in his book *History of Religions* as Hinduism being 'all things to all men' and also quoting Vincent A. Smith as saying, "The foreigners, like their forerunners the Sakas and the Yeuh-chi, universally yielded to the wonderful assimilative powers of Hinduism, and rapidly became Hinduised."[1] Atal Bihari Vajpayee, on the other hand defines India by describing it as *Bharat Ek Jeeta Jagta Rashtrapurush* (literal translation being India as a Living Legend).

Analysing the thoughts of these great men, I believe that it's not only religion that they talk about but India as a whole because this land is a hybrid thought (way of thinking) based upon the Hindu concept of coexistence that has evolved throughout its existence. By way of definition, this country is thus not a place with a demarcated border, but is a fusion achieved through centuries of assimilation.

The introduction of foreigners does not necessarily destroy the nation, they merge in it. A country is one nation only when such a condition obtains in it. That country must have a faculty for assimilation; India has ever been such a country."

—Mahatma Gandhi in his book,
Hind Swaraj (Indian Home Rule)

While closely analysing Mahatma Gandhi, Vincent A Smith, and Jawaharlal Nehru's descriptions of India's innate assimilation powers in their celebrated early works, I couldn't help but run parallels with *Star Trek's Borg Collective* (written and developed by Star Trek executive producer, Maurice Hurley). If you are a science fiction enthusiast, then Gene Roddenberry created *Star Trek: The Next Generation* (produced and distributed by Paramount Domestic Television) will most definitely be one of your favourites.

For those of you who are unfamiliar with science fiction, I will save you technical jargon, but I believe that certain concepts in the Star Trek universe have a great deal of significance to how India has been, is and will be in the future. When people ask me about India's demographic traits, I encourage them to watch Star Trek, particularly the scenes pertaining to the 'Borg' when they ask me about the demographic characteristics of India. For those not in the know, the Borg is the most petrifying yet sublime idea in the Star Trek universe. The Borg is a race of extra-terrestrial beings that do not belong to particular species or a planet but are formed through assimilation of several species. What binds together the Borg is a singular collective (Borg Collective) that has been created by synthesizing several species. Ultimately, through this assimilation exercise, the Borg relentlessly inducts new technology and new species into its collective—moving towards perfection.

I think that in the real world, not in the same format as followed by the Borg, India has been, is and will remain a synthesis of the global community (If not galactic!) seamlessly inducting newer people, ways of thinking and technologies throughout its existence.

Even though, the concept of 'India' as a country is relatively new and is a British concoction, the idea of 'Bharat Varsha' has existed for thousands of years. These values were to this land what the concept of *Westphalian Sovereignty* was for modern Europe after 1648, and that which spawned the very principle of the 'national state'. Right from the dawn of the Indian Civilisation, there have been several *rajyas* in the region, but they were all bound by a singular value system based on the ideals propounded by the forefathers of the *Bharat Varsha*.

Contrary to the belief of religious unity of the time, Hinduism is too vast a concept to be standardised as a religion, and thus Hinduism can be classified as a value system based on which people of the time lived, although the Hindu Thought was still evolving. Evolving, because in India, the influx of different cultures has always occurred and the different ways of thinking seamlessly merged into one singular hybrid thought; this is the beauty of what India represents as a country. To explain this further, I will discuss a brief epoch of Indian history. I will not talk about the time frame before the first century AD because, I feel, the most interesting period of modern Indian demographic and cultural evolution happened after it. I think that the period following the first century is the most interesting because it was a time when India was under significant influences of the Hindu, Buddhist, Islamic, Christian, Sikh, Jain, Zoroastrian, Jewish, indigenous Chinese, aborigine South East Asian and Hellenic (Greek) thoughts—all at the same time! This interesting period was the timeframe when the India Collective gained the most because under several subsequent monarchies, who ruled India over the period after it, brought in newer variations to the Collective.

Before going into detail, in order to explain several ways of thinking and eventually the India Collective, it is important to discuss it through religion, which will actually play an important role in our understanding. I believe that a thought (as part of a value system) has the power to influence masses, who then imbibe that thought into their general day-to-day living. Consequently, a religion can be explained as an evolution of a simple value system that has the power to influence established ways of thinking, in other words people of a rival value system. Every powerful and influencing religion started with the success achieved by a particular value system. Also, we must understand that the success/spread of a religious thought or eventually a particular value system has always been dependent on the assistance and patronage provided by a certain region's prominent ruling elite, who must have first understood the reasonability of a nascent thought themselves. All religions have relied on their political clout throughout their histories to spread their wings and influence adjacent regions.

This is precisely how the India Collective was formed. The main reason why the India Collective became an evolved into an eternal hybrid idea is that the region was ruled by several dynasties and cultures promoting specific value systems to the same set of people over and over again for centuries. Even the Indian people evolved genetically because of continuous influx of newer and diverse gene pools.

India's foreign policy, like that of other great regions during these years, pertained to the spread of a value system (religion). As the Apostles from West Asia were essential in the development of Christianity, the foreign policy of a prominent Indian dynasty at the time was primarily focused on using its power to disseminate intellectual ideas/thoughts associated with specific ideologies. Just as the Apostles from West Asia were instrumental in the spread of Christianity, the foreign policy of prominent Indian monarchy of the time was primarily to use its influence to spread the intellectual ideas/ thoughts pertaining to certain ideologies it were best convinced about. Studying the various monarchies and the ruling elite of India through the centuries, it is evident that the spread of a value system (later religion in this context) was primarily a monarch's spiritual influence over his subjects and beyond. Repeat if I may, spiritual influence was more important for an Indian King than mere military subjugation as spiritual influence was equivalent to total submission of the conquered people. An expert on India, author Axel Michaels aptly describes the 'Principle of Reformation of the Territorial System' (The religion of the territory is the religion of the ruler) in his book *Hinduism: Past and Present* and that precisely describes India's consistent religious reorganisations.

As a result, the people of India were forced to be adaptable to new ways of thinking because their changing monarchs wanted them to be so and there were serious ramifications for those who did not imbibe. Left with no option but to abide by the vagaries of their kings and conquerors, the citizenry therefore evolved the idea of religion into a specific value system, which continuously evolved. There is no country or region in the world where so much new thought (in varying intensities) was introduced in a span of just 1600 years of history. Little wonder that a modern Indian feels at home almost anywhere in the world. Our adaptability is remarkable to any new way of thinking. We are therefore not facing the effects of globalising now in the twenty-first century but are in fact a product of an ongoing globalisation process for centuries.

The Process of Global Convergence

The first major introduction of a new thought/ideal (way of thinking) to the Indian Collective post first century AD was the Kushana thought. The Kushana Empire (60-375 AD) brought a new value system to the India Collective through new languages and modus operandi. After their defeat at the hands of mainland China's Hsiung-nu around 177 BC (*Robert Bracey: A Rough Guide to Kushan History*) the Kushanas (early Yeuh-chi people sometimes related to the Tocharian family) were displaced from Central China and invaded Bactrian lands (present-day Northern Afghanistan) towards the beginning of the first century for settlement. It is clear that the Kushanas had lived in the Chinese mainland for centuries, sometimes even intermingling with the indigenous populations and represented a hybrid culture. Therefore, evidence does point out the fact that they must have been significantly influenced by ancient/indigenous Chinese beliefs and culture. Being a genetic fusion of Indo-European and Mongoloid descent, the Kushana influence over India also had traces of Manichaeism due to their presence on the Silk Route, a major trading route, which acted as a confluence for the exchange of Western–Eastern value systems.

Being influenced by books such as William Woodthorpe Tarn's *The Greeks in Bactria and India*, what intrigues me is the fact that the submission of the precedent Greek–Bactrian Kingdoms to the

Kushanas and the assimilation of their thought, beliefs and culture, Hellenised the Kushanas which subsequently caused their culture to become a fusion that not only included Hinduism, traces of Manichaeism and other regional beliefs but also significant Greek influences. The Buddhist thought too was significantly spread by the Kushana kings, especially the revered Emperor Kanishka, who despite using Greek as one of his court languages, appointed religious Buddhist advisors to his royal court. The consequent hybrid value system of the Kushana influence over India was thus an exotic mixture of several other value systems from the fringes of East Europe to Far East Asia and Mongolia.

Following closely and tracing its lineage to even before the Kushanas, the Maha-Meghavahana Dynasty (200 BC-400 AD) was primarily responsible for the spread of the Jain value system in India. One of the dynasty's most prominent kings, Kharavela even engaged in wars for the ultimate establishment of the Jain ideals and ultimately becoming the custodian of peace (non-violence) in the east-central India. In fact, in his book, *Life Force: The World of Jainism,* Michael Tobias argues, "Kharavela was both a Jain ruler and a military victor. But it is significant that there is no mention of his having ever killed an enemy. The conqueror used benign means, apparently, to force the will of his opponents and eventually devoted all of his time to serving Jain monks." This military doctrine became so well entrenched in Indian war strategy that it eventually influenced a convergent military stance for India in the 20th and 21st centuries, but more on that later in this book.

It should be understood that the Jain value system like the Buddhist value system has its core values derived from non-violence and respect for life (*Karma* doctrine). It was this reason why the concept of Mahatma Gandhi's Nonviolence Movement was so easily accepted in twentieth-century India because the Indian people were already conditioned to it. It is clear that the India Collective had already assimilated the concept of non-violence almost 1800 years earlier. The far-reaching influence of newer variations on the India

Collective is surprising and significant because the prominent Hindu way of thinking never talks about non-violence in the same breath as Dharma itself. Therefore, in all probability, this thought was inducted into the larger Indian Collective after Kharavela and was then passed down through generations becoming one of the principal ingredients of the India Collective. I present the Jain values following Kushana because I feel that the Jain value system following its incorporation into the India Collective, continues as a separate thinking process continuously evolving through deeper spiritual empirical research.

Subsequent to the Kushana and the Maha-Meghavahana contributions to the Indian Collective, the most important synthesis occurred somewhere in the fourth and the fifth centuries with the advent of the Gupta Dynasty (320-500 AD). Gupta India may have seen its best period of spiritually-induced intellectual advancement during what is believed to as the first authentic Indian Renaissance. What is more interesting is the fact that the Gupta Dynasty was the first major secular dynasty in India. Even though, various studies have pointed out the dynasty's religious affiliations towards Hinduism, the Buddhist and Jain value systems were given a free reign and sometimes even promoted by the royalty. As a result of these prolific conditions, the prominent Hindu thought closely associated itself with the Buddhist thought and there was a symbiotic coexistence for a period under the Guptas. This was a beginning of a major synthesis of the Hindu and Buddhist value systems in the Classical Period preceding the India Collective's next course of evolution, one of the most important evolutions yet. The dynasty patronised both Buddhist and Hindu value systems and the seed of their fusion was laid— contrary to popular belief, Hellenised (Greek-influenced) Buddhist thought (Post Kushanas) did not perish in India; it simply fused with the Hindu value system that was reinvigorated by proactive Brahmin monks winning citizens back to the dominant Hindu fold.[2] A prominent authority on Buddhism and ancient eastern cultures, Peter Harvey, explains this convergence theory in detail in his book *An Introduction to Buddhism: Teachings, History and Practices.*

Here Harvey discusses how Adi Shankaracharya, a Hindu monk and philosopher pivotal in Hinduism's revival, borrowed several facets from Buddhism and incorporated them into mainstream Hinduism as his strategy for revitalising the Hindu thought and ideals.

Another interesting explanation comes from the acclaimed webpage, *The Flow of History, A Dynamic and Graphical Approach to Teaching History,* where historian Chris Butler mentions, "Meanwhile the Brahmins were renewing contact with the people and winning many converts to their religion, which at this point had evolved into what we now call Hinduism." As a result of this amalgamation, Indian Hinduism today has grown into a synthesis of Sanatana Dharma–Buddhist value systems. The following reign of Harshavardhana, a prominent Buddhist king, proved to be a fertile ground for the assimilation of Hindu–Buddhist thoughts and ideals as well. Eventually, towards the end of the eighth century, the India Collective primarily composed of the Sanatana Dharma–Hellenic–Buddhist Fusion value system (example of Sun worship being an import and the Sun god's very 'non-Indian' attire and chariot) with the Jain ideals acting as a catalyst.

Ahimsa as a concept serves a great purpose in defining the union of these two sublime thought processes. I think, those who have read the concept of Hinduism will agree when I say that Hinduism's tryst with the directives of *Ahimsa* (Nonviolence) and *Dharma* (upholding entrusted work) is in a constant state of conflict, with the latter prevailing supreme when war has a moral justification to it. In essence, the Hindu value system predominantly talks about Dharma and the attainment of it by all means; the mention of *Ahimsa*, first defined in the *Yajur Veda* as a concept ceases to pose any threat to Dharma if war or cruelty is inflicted upon by a 'wicked' enemy. The reason why the Hindu value system became more sterile and somewhat less aggressive after the first century was simply because of its fusion with the Buddhist ideals and a significant influence from the Jain way of thinking.

"India is the motherland of our race, and Sanskrit the mother of European languages: She was the mother of our philosophy; the mother through the Arabs, of much of our mathematics; through the Buddha, of the ideals embodied in Christianity; mother, through the village community, of self-government and democracy. Mother India is in many ways the mother of us all."

—Will Durant, Historian

Southern India, on the other hand, though ensconced solely in the Hindu value system in its purest form, started to experience the new percolation thought processes from the North and West and its mainstream thought evolved as well. The Sangam era empires and subsequently other Southern empires were the first to have contact with the Muslim Arabs and Christians as early as fourth and sixth centuries. Interestingly, India was one of the original recipients of Christianity and that happened as early as the first century AD with the entry of Thomas the Apostle in present-day Tamil Nadu.[3] Later, Western Europeans too entered India through the gateways of the Southern Regions, with Portuguese from present-day Kerala, the French from present-day Tamil Nadu and the British from present-day Tamil Nadu as well. Therefore, just like the evolution of the India Collective in the North, the South was contributing its equal share.

There were several kingdoms to the south of River Narmada that became extremely influential after the first century AD and many empires such as the Chalukyas, Pandyas, Cheras, Rashtrakutas and Pallavas (spread between the third and thirteenth centuries AD) are worth a mention for their important contributions. As an example, much before the conquest of North-Western India by Mohammad bin Qasim (Emir of the Umayyad Caliphate) in the eighth century, Islam had already established itself in the India Collective—with the first Arab trader colonies (Omani Colonies, as they were called) coming up along the Malabar coastline (present-day Kerala) in as early as seventh century AD. While the assimilation of several foreign and indigenous ways of thinking was happening in the South, the spread of the Hindu thought (which was different to the heavily Buddhist–Hindu Fusion Thought prevalent in North India) occurred in South East Asia during the peak of the Chola period (8th-13th centuries); the influence of the Shri Vijaya Empire (spanning the present-day territories of Thailand, Indonesia, Singapore and Malaysia) is especially important in this argument. What resulted during this period of Southern conquests and exploits of South East Asia was remarkable; even though the spread of the Hindu ideals was paramount for the Cholas, there was significant intertwining between local value systems, which influenced the India Collective as new ways of thought started to percolate back from the South East.

There was a certain Buddhist influence in Indo-China as the Pala Empire, centred in present-day Bengal, had already started its propagation in the region through present-day Myanmar. So, as a result of all this influence, India received back a Hindu thought that was an enriched version of the original ideals spread out by the Cholas as it synthesised with the version already practiced by local (Hindu–Buddhist) empires of the regions. An analogy is seen in the twenty-first century India—the Bhojpuri (Bihari) culture that India exported to Trinidad and Tobago (Caribbean) in the sixteenth to seventeenth centuries is now coming back, albeit as hybrid Bhojpuri culture. The Caribbean Bhojpuri flavour in Anurag Kashyap's *Gangs of Wasseypur* lead soundtrack is a resounding example of the versatility of the India Collective.

Not out of action completely, West India (present-day Saurashtra in Maharashtra/Gujarat), was witnessing the advent of another major value system from present-day Iran and Turkmenistan following the death of the last Sassanid King Yazdegerd III in the late seventh century. The advent of Zoroastrianism in the ninth century, with several inflows of early settlers, is yet another extremely important epoch in Indian history. The subsequent assimilation of the Zoroastrian thought from Central Asia and Persia (present-day Iran) into the India Collective is aptly described in the sixteenth-century narration *Qissa-i-Sanjan*, which talks about the arrival and eventual settlement of the Zoroastrian thought. Arriving and then initially settling in Sanjan (in present-day Gujarat), the Zoroastrian community (now known as the Parsi community), has been involved (and is still active) in the advancement of the India Collective for over 1000 years and has given India several luminaries in the field of industry, science, technology and the arts. The community's unparalleled success is solely attributed to its seamless integration into the larger India Collective and focus on its advancement.

Meanwhile, in North West India, with the establishment of the Umayyad Caliphate territories followed by the Abbasid Caliphate, Islam was firmly established and was indigenised enough to be part of the larger India Collective. After several incursions by Muslim rulers, the final organisation of Islam as a major religion in India happened during the period of the Delhi Sultanate that conquered much of North and East India between the thirteenth and sixteenth centuries. It was further strengthened by the sixteenth- century conquests of Babur (from the House of Timur) and the eventual establishment of the Mughal Empire in India. As a result, Islam brought about an immense artistic, technological and strategic impetus to the India Collective and can be easily considered as a brand new way of thinking for India. It was a breath of fresh air just before the modern India Collective began to take shape. Such was Islam's influence over the India Collective that, more than 1200 years later, a twentieth-century India could have well become an important centre of the Islamic world as well. With the marriage of Ottoman Princess Durru Shehvar to Prince Azam Jah of Hyderabad State in the year 1931, Indian Islam became a major influencing force in the world. Princess Durru Shehvar was the daughter of Caliph Abdul Mejid II, the last official Caliph of the Islamic World, and when she married Nizam Osman Ali Khan's son, India was recognised as a major centre of Islam.

As the second-last major South Indian Empire, the Chola Empire, started to extinguish towards the end of the thirteenth century and with the advent of Islam, the North Indian and South Indian versions of the Hindu ideals somehow intermingled in a bid to strengthen the Hindu way of thinking against the threat from a new religion and thus modern Hinduism was born (categorised as a single value system by the new rulers of India). As Islam became dominant, early Islamic rulers realised the difficulty of ruling over a expansive swathe of land with diverse cultures. Achievements did not come until they actually synthesised their way of thinking with the India Collective, producing a hybrid Islamic–Hindu value system; Emperor Akbar the Great followed by Emperor Jahangir are said to be the pioneers of the concept. Until the late seventeenth century, the Mughals flourished and the new India Collective comprising Islamic-Hindu-Buddhist value systems had a brilliant confluence, making India the largest economy and the wealthiest country in the world,[4] continuing the achievements of the classical era. However, the Mughal Empire slowly deteriorated towards the end of the seventeenth century due to inter-clan rivalries. Additionally, there was a constant opposition from the Hindu Maratha Empire (1674-1820 AD), which was now much stronger and more integrated. It was founded by the great Maratha Emperor Chhatrapati Shivaji, who is well known for his heroic efforts to keep India united after the end of the Mughal era. The Marathas were also known to be the last Hindu rulers of India until the British arrived and became politically dominant.

Following the Marathas' defeat in the Third Anglo–Maratha War in 1818, the British became India's dominant rulers, and Western thought and ultimately value systems permeated India subtly through the English language, Christianity's association with Western-style education and the concept of social elitism. The Western way of thinking percolated into the rigid Indian caste system, where the concept of 'aspiration' was inculcated and the age-old caste-based social isolation was destroyed.

It must be noted that the British prominence over India was a by-product of an unprecedented European interest in India over a considerable period of time, starting with the establishment of several East India Companies by European nations from the fifteenth through seventeenth centuries after the arrival of the Portuguese—Vasco da Gama—at Calicut (Kerala). The Danish, the Portuguese, the British, the Dutch and the French were all here and there was a significant Modern European influence over India and slowly the post-European Renaissance Western way of thinking made inroads into the India Collective. Nevertheless, the British East India Company, the most successful in India among its counterparts, was harbouring megalomaniac ambitions and knew that the only way it could integrate and control an Indian Empire was by destroying the India Collective, resulting in the formulation of its infamous Divide and Rule Policy.

What resulted from this faulty way of thinking was the destruction of the social fabric of India and the emergence of permanent divisions between the Hindu and the Islamic value systems. Also, I think that the painful episode of partition in Indian history mainly happened because of the British apathy towards integrating the Hindu and the Islamic value systems. What was seamlessly achieved in Akbar's reign was destroyed during Aurangzeb's and then the British, as the new rulers of India did not bother to reunite them probably because of their own vested interests and preoccupations in trying to rule a vast swathe of unchartered territory.

On a positive note though, the European advent exposed India to a new liberal Christian ideals and values, which were one of liberalisation and brought about acceptance of foreign values as something advantageous to imbibe rather than forced (examples are the use of the English language for one's own benefit and the disbandment of Indian orthodox beliefs such as Sati). Eventually, towards the end of the nineteenth century and early twentieth century, the India Collective mainly comprised of three independent primary value systems—the hybrid Sanatana Dharma (Hindu), the liberal Christian and the Islamic value systems. The Jain and the Sikh ideals continued to influence the Collective through their spiritual evolutions throughout these years.

India, therefore, today is thus processing vast stimuli to which it has been continuously introduced for centuries; contrarily, it is certainly not in a state of confusion. With so much assimilation and evolution, the India Collective has become an all-encompassing 'Convergent Thought' process that continues to expand, as often pointed out by Member of Parliament and former Cabinet Minister

Shashi Tharoor in his speeches. This convergence, however, does not make India an introvert nation but a self-contained nation that is content with what it has because it has the entire world's culture and ideals within it.

As a country, India is striving towards unity—spiritually and, ultimately, scientifically. The collective in India centrally revolves around spirituality and it is very different to that of the United States, whose collective though a hybrid like India is based more on national superiority and pride (Achievers Club). Most readers may not agree and will cite all the present ambiguities (the legendary Indian chaos) but then these are transitional times. We must understand that so much new thought has been introduced to this region that a little over 70 years is not sufficient for the mental processing to take place. For the first time in 2000 years, the Indian people have the opportunity to govern themselves without an introduction of a newer value system (in any case, none is left out).

After all this hoopla and interesting times, one thing is for sure—once the processing is complete, what will emerge from this confusion will be a Collective that will be absolute and all-encompassing.

"A nation's strength ultimately consists in what it can do on its own, and not in what it can borrow from others."

—Indira Gandhi,
Former Prime Minister of India

What India Actually is Today

Story of economics, consumerism, inflation, interest rate, food, movies and the love lost...

What Drives India?

Taking the last chapter forward, I think the best way to understand the **Collective** is to understand the way it functions today in a twenty-first century environment. Interestingly, there is an underlying alpha thought doing the rounds here and I suspect this is something that really drives India; strangely enough, we the citizens are subconsciously connected to our collective, whether we are aware of it or not. When you read further, you will see how India actually inducts the best thoughts into its fold even today. Surprisingly, everything is seamlessly connected in a mesh of disparate thoughts.

The Process of Integration

I think the best way to understand this process of integration in India is to analyse what goes on at our very own cigarette/*chai* stalls, omnipresent in every Indian neighbourhood. The current Prime Minister, Narendra Modi, and perhaps India's most revered leader of the twenty-first century, proudly states that he once was a '*chai* vendor'; Narendra Modi's reverence towards this métier is not without a reason because in the success of the India Collective, these vendors have aided tremendously by becoming the centre points/ hoarders of mass opinion. The media hype around *chaiwallas* during the 2014 general elections proves this point.

These cigarette/*chai* stalls are the hallmark of our democracy, acting as mini parliaments of sorts, where the people can talk about virtually anything to their heart's content. We are a spiritual bunch of people and we must understand that India survives through a catharsis of thought. An average Indian basks in the glory of his argumentative nature and actually his/her spiritual well-being depends on the ability of winning a coveted discussion. Also, I think these stalls are the all-important 'confluence nodes of the Indian thought (read: India Collective)'. Just like the Darwinian Theory of Natural Selection, the best thoughts/ideas/ideals among all thoughts survive and travel from one cigarette stall to the other and eventually to homes from where it has the power to influence this nation single-handedly. Such 'alpha thoughts' that are inculcated through these nodes are the binders or destroyers of this nation—no matter which way you look at them. You might agree that the power of such thoughts (positive ones of course) has saved India from the various civil unrests which might have engulfed the nation at various lows of our struggling history. Precisely this is what the India Collective is all about; a combination of alpha thoughts eventually influencing us in our everyday functioning.

Clearly, these positive alpha thoughts are the messenger molecules of our democratic setup today. The economic liberalisation and the following material gains and choices, for instance, were such positive conversation starters that brought about a sense of positivity in a nation bereft of avenues for feel-good conversations. This is how the integration and further evolution of the India Collective is happening as the country's dynamic value system inducts our best thoughts/ affirmative actions/ideals continuously and presents them as if they were part of our own gene pool.

The Fiscal Side of Things

I think that before liberalisation, India could survive 44 years as an entity not only because of a great deal of euphoria of being a free nation (a feeling that was part of an entire generation's belief system), but also because of the Plan Policy framework and the concept of self-sufficiency. I vividly remember asking my teacher, Ms. Pradhan, what it means to be self-sufficient while we were studying a chapter of Indian history in Class 7. To which she replied that it's all about being independent in every way possible. Even though, what Ms. Pradhan said was a fairly simple explanation to a question, her answer went a long way in actually defining my way of thinking and identity as an Indian. The concept of self-sufficiency then is what every Indian aspired to achieve post-Independence in 1947 and interestingly it represents something about who we are. We must understand that the concept of *Swadesi* (homegrown), a direct consequence of the *Satyagraha* movement propounded by Mahatma Gandhi, is part of our psyche and is already ingrained in our value system.

A number of analysts blame the British for the Indian obsession pertaining to self-sufficiency, and the former's way of reasoning is quite simple to understand. You see, India never required the services of the East India Company in the first place; when it came anyway, it was allowed to be present on the Indian homeland purely for business. Profiteering was, however, not the primary motive of the 'Company' and it ended up ruling the Indian masses for over 250 years. Figuratively speaking, it was nothing but a Multinational Corporation (MNC) that subdued the Indian pride of self-governance and destroyed the credibility of the established Indian value system based on diversity.

India, throughout its history has welcomed and assimilated every man/woman with open arms; such is India's diversity and openness that Indians were proud of this fact. However, when entities such as the East India Company reneged on their promises, differences and scepticism appeared permanently. We must understand the fact that the British came to India as entrepreneurs, and not as conquerors. This schism became even more pronounced after the Bhopal Gas Tragedy in December 1984, which affected over 500,000 people. Apathy and a near-cold response from the responsible MNC—

America's Union Carbide—established the belief that MNCs are equal to conspiracies against poor people and that they are façades merely to protect conniving and despicable individuals masquerading as 'Company' representatives.

Regrettably, this attitude persists among the Indian populace. Due to early instances of such anomalies caused by 'Companies', as they are derogatorily referred to by Indians, the image of large private entities became unpopular and untrustworthy in the Indian grand scheme of things. Private businessmen and entrepreneurs still face hostility in daily affairs so much so that their modus operandi is often under public scrutiny. Resultantly, India has become one of the few countries in the world that does not respect its wealth creators, who instead become fodder for gossip and are discounted on grounds of lacking morality. As a consequence it became even more attractive to have a model in which large business entities are collectively owned by the public and so constrained by public sentiment and its well-being. At the end of the day, the purpose of a public-owned company is service and not profit. Self-reliance is, therefore, a belief that stems from self-governance and public service.

India as an economic entity has always been a self-reliant country, economically depending on very little import through its history of being a trading nation. The country actually was the largest economy in the world (until its decline in the 18th century) just because of its status as a net exporter (much like today's Germany, Japan and China). Our economy did not become import dependent until the British arrived (a transition that occurred as a result of India's British-led strategic concentrate on being a main feeder and consumer of the emerging industrial revolution in the UK). Therefore, in all probability India was not self-sufficient only in between the times the British came and left, i.e., about 250 years (roughly). It is part of the India Collective to be self-reliant, and Pandit Nehru's vision of an India getting back to its roots was all but a natural course of action. Nehru realised early on that the Government must take a leadership position to steer newly independent India into the direction where lies its destiny; in order for this to happen the state must presume the position of a 'father figure.' According to Harvard Business School Professor Richard H.K. Vietor's book *How Countries Compete, Strategy, Structure and Governmentin the Global Economy*, "A Democratic Socialist, and admirer of the Soviet Union, Nehru believed that state planning should allocate scarce investment resources. In 1948, the government issued its industrial policy resolution, giving government exclusive authority over railroads, telecommunications, power and the postal system."

Arguably, Nehru and his advisors, it seems, were also highly influenced by the American model of economic welfare and sustenance post the Great Depression of 1931—one of the most effective follow-ups to '*The New Deal*'. As the Democrats (often termed as the custodians of the so called 'Liberal' thought) enacted the '*Wagner Act*', which massively brought about public welfare through government spending, it so appeared that a free market eco-system with a determined state can do a decent job in preserving an ailing economy. As a result, Nehru felt it was safe to include not just a socialist perspective, but also a fairly constrained capitalist perspective when he envisioned the structures of the Indian economy. This middle path led to a confluence of thoughts and spawned the so-called mixed economy model in which even though market forces were free to interact, the state was concurrent and the domestic industry was a priority. Not without reason, depending very little on the rest of the world, India is conditioned to be a true domestic demand-driven economy—a feat that very few other economies have managed to achieve in so little time.

As a modern twenty-first-century economy, India is reaping the rewards of being a somewhat closed economy for close to 40 years because the time gave India an opportunity to introspect and to look within, finding what it can do with itself. While I agree with the fact that the period was not very conducive as far as startups are concerned (especially the point pertaining to ease of doing business), but what emerged from the quagmire of License Raj, Protectionism of Industry and Lack of Consumer Choice was a resilient Indian economy capable of competing with the rest of the world. A classic example is a comparison with the Pakistani economy, which started out being richer in terms of per capita than India but eventually lost out because it never really incubated its nascent industry from foreign competition, leaving it with no cutting-edge, globally competitive industry at all (except maybe cotton and textile) towards the end of the twentieth century. India, on the other hand, found itself in a sweet spot when it opened its economy because Indian industry covered almost all sectors present in a modern economy and was able to effectively partner with foreign corporations (rather than competing head on), resulting in a win-win situation. By the time India was a liberalised and an open economy, the industry spawned several Fortune 500 (and rivalling) private sector stalwarts such as the Tata Group, Reliance, Birla Groups, Bajaj Group, L&T, Godrej, Mahindra, Infosys, Kalyani Group, Bharti Airtel, Wipro and many others—proof enough that India gained more than it lost because of its policy pertaining to self-sufficiency. However, the establishment of these mega corporations was hugely facilitated by 'father figure' government enterprises, which is another side of our story on self-sufficiency that led to Co-operation rather than Collision.

If we closely analyse the Indian industry in general, it is clear that the industrial frameworks on which India has built its economy are based on Public Sector Undertakings (government-owned enterprises). Companies (sorry, industries!) such as SAIL, ONGC, SBI, IOC, BHEL, HAL, DRDO, Maruti Udyog (now Maruti Suzuki) and many other so-called offspring of the 'Nehruvian Consensus' have given the Indian economy the foundation to stand tall and build further successes (even though there are instances where private sector has supplemented the government's effort). Interestingly, the development and incubation of these public organisations has been done through public money (what you and I deposit in the banks) and not cheaper foreign credit (and consequent ultra-low foreign debt to GDP ratio)—a fact that furthers my argument of self-sufficiency because dependence on public money is something that the government inherently found safe and dependable; inherently because it is our psychological belief (and the government is today run by the society's representatives and not foreigners).

The nationalisation of major Indian banks in the year 1969 is a case in point here. When India quietly nationalised 14 large commercial banks, while it was a surprising decision, nonetheless it was an apt example of securing self-sufficiency at all costs. I believe the decision was a direct reaction to the nationalisations of Cuba instigated by Fidel Castro in the year 1960. Even though Castro's model of business was through an absolute state control (unlike the Indian model), both nationalisation exercises were prompted by insecurity as banks were the central financiers to the predominantly state-'piloted' economies and then-Prime Minister Indira Gandhi knew her economics well.

Therefore, instruments such as high interest rates along with a high Cash Reserve Ratio (CRR) and Statutory Liquidity Ratio (SLR) (a portion of Net Demand and Time Liability (NDTL) in the form of government bonds and hedging commodities such as gold) are prevalent in India simply because Government expenditure depends on public money and the monetary policy always must adjust because that is sacrosanct (not a job). Even though prior to and after nationalisation the CRR and an unreal SLR (fixed by an amended Banking Regulation Act 1962 at 25 percent but now gradually coming down to below 20 percent level) have remained tools to control liquidity in the system and maintain a safety net for commercial banks, choosing to go overboard in lending, there is a bigger picture to it. Believe it or not, it seems, the RBI considers it its moral duty to finance government spending. The modern Indian economy is based on the state being the primary provider to the Indian people; the state's status is almost like that of a father figure in India and therefore even though it is the function of the monitory policy to adjust to the fiscal movements, it seems in India it is the former's moral responsibility. What else explains why, in a country where over 69 percent of public deposits are held in nationalised banks, a minimal reserve requirement is prevalent when standard sterilization tools can do the trick? To understand how the monetary and fiscal sides interact, we must understand the relationship between the central bank and the government first, but that is a different topic altogether.

Therefore, the argument of the fiscal side rests on the fact that we Indians save not because the Indian state does not provide welfare services or the monetary policy is faulty, but because we are conditioned to be self-sufficient. A good example can be a modern Indian, even if he/she is a rich and successful professional, still (on an average) has a propensity to save because it offers a feeling of empowerment. This acquired psychological conditioning happened because of the several and uncertain policy frameworks and future (under several foreign rulers of India) under which we Indians had to live for generations. This is precisely why even our economic decisions are defined by the India Collective.

The Political Side of Things

What's the point of maintaining state control, you could object, now that India is a \$3.1+ trillion economy and the world's third largest economy in terms of purchasing power! Swaraj is the answer, yet another manifestation of our collectivity in action. An India that is built on cooperation.

In his book, *'Swaraj,'* which is also the basis of the political party he founded, Aam Aadmi Party (AAP), Arvind Kejriwal talks about three places in different time periods to explain his concept of Swaraj or Self Rule. He starts with the example of ancient Bharat Varsha's Vaishali kingdom, which according to his book was the world's first true democracy; then he talks about the village of Kutumbacum in Tamil Nadu and finally about the village of Hivare Bazar in Maharashtra. In all three examples, Kejriwal talks about people's 'collective action' as the means towards achieving ends. Through the empowerment of the Gram Sabha at the village level and the Residential Welfare

Associations at the urban level, he concerns himself with the fact that local governance is the most effective governance for India because the country has always had had this form of governance for centuries; a system which he says was dismantled by the British and replaced by the system of District Collectors in the mid-nineteenth century.

Kejriwal's concept of Swaraj has its roots firmly attached in the movement started by Mahatma Gandhi, who, influenced by the works of Leo Tolstoy, termed the 'monolith state' as damaging to the people and that local governance was the best way to forward public interests in terms of socio-economic well-being. Gandhi believed that self-governance or Swaraj through 'political decentralisation' will empower the common man, who will in turn have more power to decide the course of his life independently. This according to Gandhi will not only make people more self-sustaining, but will also inculcate morality among the communities.

> *"Power resides in the people; they can use it at any time."*[5]
>
> —Mahatma Gandhi

The concept of Swaraj, as per Gandhi, was a means to achieve *Moksha* (Sanskrit for liberation), and that the envisioned end was to be free of government authority and remaining so to say, independent and self-reliant. Since, the timing of this concept coincided with the fact that the country was ruled by a foreign government that acted as a barnacle and was instrumental in the destruction of the system of self-governance in its purest form—Swaraj emerged as a direct antithesis to the British rule, which focused on absolute state control. In order to achieve the objectives of Swaraj, Gandhi brought about the instrument of organised resistance, which he termed 'Non-Cooperation Movement' in order to drive the point home that his concept was based on the principle of non-violence—the Non-Cooperation Movement was synonymous with *Satyagraha* (Sanskrit for insisting on truth), which concerned itself with the demand for justice.

The concept soon became a mass movement and influencer of public sentiment; millions of Indians started practicing Satyagraha and boycotted British goods, services, education and general government rules and regulations, engulfing the entire nation in its wake. This was the progenitor of the second Indian freedom struggle after the failure of the Mutiny of 1857 and would later influence greats such as American Martin Luther King Jr. and the South African Nelson Mandela. Actually, India's resistance movement was influenced by American philosopher Henry David Thoreau in the nineteenth century, who was instrumental in conceptualising the very concept of resistance through non-cooperation with the state. The American's deep-rooted belief system in the *Bhagavad Gita* (Hindu sacred text) was also instrumental in the adaptation of this concept in India with significant indigenisation through later additions such as Satyagraha and non-violence.

The struggle was successful and by the mid-1920s, Swaraj became a political movement with several high-profile people along with the masses starting to openly practice Satyagraha, engaging in non-cooperation. The Congress Party (India National Congress) under the leadership of Jawaharlal Nehru launched the *Sampurna Swaraj* (Sanskrit for complete freedom) in the year 1929 under the aegis of Mahatma Gandhi and the British were given the referendum of the Indian people to restore power back to the natives. Swaraj or Self Rule through Non-Cooperation became the buzzword, and the Congress party established its ethos on the concept of Self Rule and portrayed itself as being the custodian of the new liberated India. After Gandhi, nationalist Jayaprakash Narayan expanded on the concept of Swaraj and was instrumental in incorporating the concept into the Indian psyche.

"Swaraj is my birthright and I shall have it!"

—Bal Gangadhar Tilak, Indian nationalist,
Indian National Congress

However, in this frenzy to establish the Indian ethos, there was another side of the Indian political movement that emerged—one with right-winged conservative attitudes and often perceived extremist tendencies: The Muslim League that later founded Pakistan, on the one hand, and the Hindu nationalist organisation, RSS, on the other. Interestingly, the origins of the RSS are also ensconced in the concept of Swaraj and self-rule, in which as a matter of fact the RSS has played a major role. A doctor form Nagpur, Maharashtra, Keshav Baliram Hedgewar—who was a Satyagrahi himself and a staunch nationalist arrested by the British in such adventures—established the Rashtriya Swayamsevak Sangh (RSS) literally meaning National Self Help and Governance Committee in 1925. Even though RSS in its early days was not an organised entity and attained such a status only in 1949 (becoming even more influential with the reorganisation under the Sangh Pariwar Collective), it had a widespread support in India, especially among the Hindus and talked about the concept of Hindu nationalism, which was later mistaken as incorporating only the Hindu people and being intolerant towards the non-Hindus. In actuality, the RSS's mission was and still is 'Selfless Service to the Motherland' and was explained by M.S. Golwalkar, the second chief of the RSS, most aptly as:

> *"RSS has been making determined efforts to inculcate the burning devotion for Bharat and its national ethos; sterling qualities and character; rouse social consciousness, mutual good-will, love and cooperation among all ... to create all round Anushasana (Sanskrit for discipline) in all walks of life and build together all our people into a unified harmonious national whole, extending from Himalayas to Kanyakumari."*[6]
>
> —MS Golwalkar, former RSS Chief

Under the stalwart leadership of Syama Prasad Mookerjee and later L.K. Advani and Atal Bihari Vajpayee, the BJP emerged as the political representation of the RSS belief system in the year 1980 and later tweaked its ideology to "*Sarva Dharma Sambhava*" (Sanskrit for respect for all religions) modifying the concept of '*Hindutva*' and broadening it to incorporate all Indians irrespective of religion. It must be pointed out that for many followers of the RSS, Hinduism is not a religion but a way of life, and rightly so.

With time, the modern Indian political landscape came to be dominated at the national level by two sides, with the liberal Centre-Left Congress on one side and the Conservative-Right BJP on the other occupying the national stage. However, as the passion of freedom struggle died down in India, the true colours of the India Collective emerged. Since this land of diversity is a land with several opinions, there was never any consensus that could be reached in its entirety. Rarely did these major dominant parties ascend to power solely on their own strength; they required the support of hundreds of regional organisations that sprang up across the country. Thus, the Coalition era began in India, and regional parties gained prominence in the political machinery.

This is a classic case of the famous 'Kuznets Curve' propounded by Economist Simon Kuznets. Recently, the concept was made popular by French Economist Thomas Piketty in his acclaimed book *Capital in the Twenty-First Century.* Kuznets states that when per capita incomes increases, inequalities decline, and that the most inequality occurs when a country reaches middle income status. As per later additions to the theory, several economists have added that as inequalities decline due to higher economic participation of a country's population, formerly marginalised people start to participate in a country's socioeconomic structures over time. Affirmative action in India over the years has assured that this has happened and people have adjusted to their new aspirations. True to their nature, the Indian people have made sure that all their interests are represented in the political jigsaw puzzle and the coalition form of 'Cooperative Governance' is the living proof of this habit. This in a way kept checks and balances in the system and allowed for a safety valve to be incorporated into governance; so to say the 'monolith state' was less intimidating. Whenever local/regional interests did not find themselves in the larger scheme of things, a regional party threatened to withdraw its support from the ruling coalition—virtually guaranteeing decentralised governance.

However, this new system of governance, though similar to self-rule, bordered the British-invented system of elected representatives that formed a 'monolith state' and again started to become a source of angst for the common man. The change from the fight against the British through the demand for Swaraj and the fight against native rulers through the demand of equality and fairness was so intense that the Indian people were almost caught in a time warp. In the emotion of fighting against a foreign government, Indians never really got out of this system and continue to practise non-cooperation against their homegrown government subconsciously; the legendary Indian chaos is a direct proof of its existence. Whether for the better or the worse, their psyche has already incorporated the concept of 'Non-Cooperation' for the attainment of Swaraj and Indians are still involved generation after generation. This has led to the emergence of Kejriwal's Aam Aadmi Party, which proclaims the establishment of Swaraj and the Indian people are hooked. Winning almost all the 70 seats in Delhi elections and until recently thousands joining every day at the national level are just a few examples of the Indian people's affinity towards collective action. The concept of Swaraj is therefore not just an idea whose time has come but a phenomenon that has been part of our very Indianness, our Collective. One only hopes that this new cohesion helps us Indians to get out of our non-cooperative attitudes and forces us to understand what real Swaraj actually means—cooperation for collective benefit.

The Car Side of Things

"I always say, the way a man treats his car is the way he treats himself."

—Officer Tarconi to Frank,

The Transporter *movie (2002)*[7]

True, isn't it? Except in our case, it should say—"The way a man buys his car is the way he buys everything else."

In a high inflation riddled economy, buying decisions are always held at ransom. Interest rates take their toll on consumption patterns and general demand invariably declines; a situation most dreaded by volume-driven companies. This may be true in most cases but apparently Maruti Suzuki is an exception to the rule. It takes a lot to surprise the market, but Maruti Suzuki always manages to flabbergast. When the company's domestic sales in October 2012 (when Auto Inc's sales were at an absolute nadir) grew by 86 percent in a market that managed to grow by only 23 percent, eyebrows were raised in all analytical circles. Here was a company reeling under severe labour unrests during recessionary market conditions yet managing to humble its competition with aplomb. During the same month, domestic sales of other major players such as Hyundai Motor India, Toyota Kirloskar and General Motors increased by just 8.5 percent, 14 percent and 32 percent respectively. Some competitors such as Tata Motors and Ford India even faced a decline as they sold 15 percent and 6.3 percent less cars respectively. Year 2014 figures were no different—in June 2014, Indian auto industry finally showed positive numbers after almost a two-year hiatus. Here too, Maruti Suzuki sales increased by an unbelievable 33 percent, when most of the market was either in negative territory or just out of the red.

Clearly, when it comes to automotive conspicuous consumption (shear volumes) in India, Maruti is the undisputed champion. Amidst fresh competition in the Indian automotive market today, even though Maruti Suzuki may not be the most coveted badge to own, it certainly is the most respected. There is a glorious history associated with Maruti's origins so much so that there is an instant connection with the nation at large. What else can explain the company's special emphasis on the market's entry (A, B, B2 and C) segments?

When Maruti Udyog was established in the year 1981, it was possibly the most ambitious undertaking undertaken by the

Government of India to date, and was realistically based on the aspirations of new India.

Maruti Udyog was a Public Sector Unit with a difference as it was associated with the glamorous topic of cars and that too from Japan, the home to the world's automotive *haute couture* of those days. Since the 80s was a time when the License Raj was at its peak, the automotive market, just like everything else was 'access controlled' and involved very little choices. As market offerings were obsolete, there was a need to bring about changes to the status quo without opening the flood gates to foreign competition. After all indigenous efforts to go about failed, the final strategy was formulated.

The plan was simple, set up a new government company in technical collaboration with an established multinational and provide affordable mobility solutions to the Indian masses. Suzuki Motor Corporation was a natural fit because it was the only company with expertise in manufacturing sub 1L (micro cars) cars at a cost none of its competition could manage. As a result of this collaboration, when the Maruti 800 was finally launched almost three years later, it was a rage, and Maruti Suzuki has never looked back since. In the next decade, the company battled in a highly competitive post-liberalisation market that involved almost all the world's major players. Surprisingly, this child of pre-liberalised India still rules the roost, garnering 45 percent of India's automotive market share within a matter of 39 years of existence. Analysts are astonished by the sales fortunes of Maruti; it's not every day that in a market characterised by perfect competition, a manufacturer's portfolio regularly dominates half of the top ten sellers' list! In September–October 2012, Maruti's six models were among the top ten sellers! Astounding because the top ten sellers' combined volume during September 2012 was just over 106,589 units, out of which 73,209 units were sold by Maruti alone. These figures indicate that Maruti held a stunning 69 percent of the market when volume is the primary parameter.

South Korean giant Hyundai Motors India and homegrown player Tata Motors are possibly the only firms who have ever come close to competing with Maruti in numerous areas, although even they could never match the latter's sheer volume. Before the battle raged in the C segment (premium hatchbacks), Maruti's primary volume driver, Alto was selling over 21,000 units per month and the competition always found the car's segment (entry level segment) difficult to crack. Stakes were high and competition was firing all cylinders to match up; attempt one was made by Tata Motors' much hyped Nano, which was a sub Rs. 200,000 car and undercut the Maruti Alto by over Rs. 90,000. The Nano had everything going in its favour and came with a promise from one of India's most respected business houses. After initial success, the Nano could not match the Alto's volume. Attempt two was taken by Hyundai Motors India with the very stylish compact Eon. Even though with the Eon, Hyundai offered a very contemporary package at a very competitive price, the model failed to dent the sales of the comparatively basic and dated Alto. To the market's surprise, both Tata Nano and Hyundai Eon did not even feature in the top ten list of September 2012! Hyundai Eon, on the other hand, made it onto the coveted list before being phased out completely.

Maruti's success has been attributed to its market foresight, model fit and customer satisfaction. What several experts appear to overlook, though, is the rationale behind consumer selection. While it is true that Maruti's product line provides significant value to the customer, the primary reason for consumer faith in Maruti products is the Indian consumer psychology. How else can one explain the continued high demand for Maruti products with waiting lists often spanning months even during the disparaging Manesar crisis? Through these times, the competition continued to offer similar products, sometimes with even better value, but surprisingly to no avail.

Evidently, when it comes to important investment decisions, the Indian consumer loves products and services that have a government assurance—pointing directly to an India imbibing the Nehruvian Consensus into its Collective. Considering the fact that an investment in a car is not just a one time major investment but that which involves several factors such as the re-sale value and long-term company reliability, cars are definitely a very important investment decision taken with extreme caution. As a parallel, if we take the example of the nationalised banks of India, they clearly outstrip private competition by a mile as well. According to RBI data of 2013, out of the total Indian deposits worth Rs. 56,16,432 crore that are deposited with commercial banks, Rs. 43,72,985 crore (almost 78 percent of total) were parked with nationalised banks alone! Even with private banks firing all cylinders in the 2010s, the ratio is still in the vicinity of 65:35. Another case of major investment decisions based on government assurance. Like cars, investing one's life savings involves a lot of assurance as well and here too government backing wins. The Indian obsession with everything *sarkari* is something that is ensconced in our mindset and influences many of our key purchasing decisions; strangely this is again a figment of the *Swadesi* mindset that has been permanently imbibed in our way of life. Even though Maruti Udyog is now Maruti Suzuki, which is now a public limited company with no government ownership whatsoever, the government-backed goodwill still psychologically persists. The fact that Maruti was established with full government backing undoubtedly has a significant impact on purchasing decisions. The reason why Tata Motors on the other hand was not able to take advantage of the *Swadesi* mindset is still nebulous but we might see a reinvigorated model line-up in the near future from the company, allowing us to witness the India Collective's imbibed values in its full splendour.

Today, as an evolved and successful company, Maruti Suzuki has stepped up its game, identifying consumer trends before competition senses a market lacuna. Maruti's products usually make their way into the customer sweet spot, owing to the company's lightning-fast adaptation to market conditions. And all this is possible not only because the company has enough volumes and technology important to go about any product evolution necessitated by the market but also by the consumer's unfaltering and unwavering confidence in the company's abilities. It's a *quid pro quo* relationship that the company enjoys with the Indian market and the best part is nobody's complaining. With a renewed vigour, Tata Motors is now trying to bring about a similar revolution of sorts enticing Indian consumer's *Swadesi* sweet spot with its recent crop of top-quality cars. These are still early days though.

The Food Side of Things

When Indian politicians say that the root cause of social evils prevalent in our society today is our changing food habits (famously, by eating Chowmien?!), there may be a couple of suppressed giggles here and there, but I think there is a great correlation with India's evolution as a society. Today, people use the terms "food" and "society" interchangeably since, as a relatively recent phenomena, food has become the latest sensation on Indian television, print and online media; no matter where you see, it's there. A lot of people argue that cookery shows have been successful everywhere in the world so India is not an exception; yet, some contend that since Indians already have so much indigenous food, which the world loves, why on earth should we be required to learn new cuisines? I think it could be out of novelty, but what if we inherently love to experiment with our food?

This is food for thought, isn't it? Well, they say that the genuine way to a man's (or a woman's) heart is through his/her stomach. If this is the case than obviously, Indians too are not stimulated by intellectual stuff alone as there has to be real food that goes to the stomach first and stimulates the mind later. If that is the case, so be it...

In his column titled "Our Jalebi Versus Their Zulabiya" in *Hindustan Times Brunch* (dated February 3, 2013) one of India's most well-known and respected journalists, Vir Sanghvi, discusses

India's accomplishment in seamlessly assimilating the world's numerous cuisines. Undoubtedly, there is a lot of truth in Mr. Sanghvi's astute analysis. There is no greater contribution to the India Collective of today than the evolution of Indian food. Clearly, Clearly, Indians' gastronomical customs have always been in motion and have never stayed static. As with the developing India Collective, the ongoing tug-of-war between fiscal and monetary policies, and the never-ending parliamentary disputes, Indian cuisine has never been truly standardised or even attempted; soya *sabzi* anyone? Cuisines such as Mughlai, Hyderabadi, Awadhi and Punjabi all have significant influences of Arabic, Persian, Turkic, Afghani and Central Asian, yet they are authentic Indian cuisines of today. Modern Indian food, like modern Indian thought, has evolved over time to reflect the way we think about ourselves today. Like I said earlier, Indian food is in a constant state of flux because we as a nation are in that state and we like to be that way. What else explains our new found competencies in information technology and heavy engineering, when the world previously dismissed us as the land of snake charmers and elephants (some still do by the way!). Our adaptability is the key to our evolution, and our food is no exception, for as we evolve, our culinary habits must keep up too.

Talking about our state of flux, I think that *Masala Chai* is the greatest example to everything that I have tried to express by wasting all these pages here. *Masala Chai*, which is the Indian version of the British-invented Tea, is a national beverage, so much so that most Indians can't think of living without their daily dose of *chai* (several doses actually). It is hard to believe that before the British arrived, the concept of *chai* was a non-existent one in India and within 250 years it has seamlessly integrated into the India Collective. Western-style confectionaries are another good example of how our food has changed. Feel-good foods such as pastries, bun, rusk and cookies are something that go along with the local *namkeens* of India and complement the evening or morning tea for most Indians. What I'm referring to is spotting a local *chai* vendor with just a stove in a homemade tent beside a construction site, serving rusk/cookie along with tea to daily wage earners. For a daily wage earner, it really doesn't matter where the rusk (popular variant Helicopter)/cookie originated from because for him/her it is as Indian as *chai* itself is. The best part about Indian food is that when it assimilates a new type of gastronomical influence, there is a significant indigenisation of it. *Chai* itself is a pretty indigenised version of the Tea that is available in the western world, as the typical '*Masala Chai*' (Indian Tea) is extremely milky and sweet. Chinese cuisine for example represents another significant indigenisation before its integration into the Indian Collective. The Chinese food that we have here is vastly different from the authentic Chinese that one gets in the Chinese mainland. I know this because I received a harsh awakening in China when I anticipated eating the Chinese food that I regularly eat at a roadside stall in India.. For those, who have never been to China or experienced authentic Chinese food, I can assure them that there is nothing in India that can prepare you for what is available in China (in the name of food). I don't intend to offend Chinese gastronomical habits but the street Chinese food that we get in India is heavily Indianised and that is India's way of induction. Of course, the large Indo-Chinese community of Kolkata has a major role to play in making Chinese food a household name in India. Another example is the high popularity of Goan food, which is heavily influenced by the Portuguese, in connoisseur circles.

Evolution is thus an inevitability and we Indians take it for granted, and therefore the alpha thoughts that originate in places where people come together (temporarily or permanently) to relax and discuss trivial issues (ranging from small talks, politics of development to sometimes even foreign policy) are what make social conscience and help form or break public consensus. Importantly these thoughts evolve, like everything else. Food for thought then; our evolving food is an important side of the modern India we know today and we cannot sabotage the evolution of our thought by standardising our food. Speaking of which, a more recent phenomenon is the popularity and integration of Tibetan cuisine in India with the advent of Tibetans into the country some 40 years ago. While the Tibetan people of India have not completely integrated into Indian culture, distancing themselves from the Indian Collective, their way of existence has percolated into the Indian mainstream. Tibetan foods have recently become the most popular street food available in India, and among urban youngsters it often even outperforms indigenous Indian variants such as '*chat*' (*gol gappe*, *tikki*, *bhalle*, *pav bhaji*, *bhel puri*, etc). In main course too, Tibetan cuisines such as *Momo* and *Thukpa* are as much Indian today as is *Dosa Sambhar*, *Chole Chawal* or *Dal Roti*. Italian and Mexican foods are other examples, but then I can go on and on and on; however, there is no need because we understand the underlying concept anyway.

In light of these new developments and integrations, one can't help but admire the maturity of the Indian Collective and its ability to connect with what the world has to offer. When the so called modern Western civilisations are turning extremely xenophobic and banning non-Western ways, India has continuously accepted and absorbed newer versions of life as its own.

The Movie Side of Things

If you want to see the changing face of the India Collective, Live, you have to see the changing face of Bollywood (The Bombay Film Industry). Bollywood then, describes the evolving Indian society most aptly. In my opinion, Ashutosh Gowariker's 2008 hit movie, *Jodhaa Akbar*, is the true representation of India. The reason why such stories intrigue us is because a confluence culture is part of our psyche. The movie's success was not dependent on a figment of chance, but our psychological programming, our collective.

During my business journalism days in New Delhi, Sutanu Guru, one of India's senior business journalists and author of the acclaimed book *Beyond Rahul Vs Modi (2014-2024: The Battle for*

India's Soul) used to often talk about how all writers analysing India should take inspiration from Bollywood and its evolution through the movies that come out of there. According to him, Bollywood has a different theme in every decade as the movies evolve with time and the prevalent situation of the country. Examples may include the changing face of the villain. Until the 1970s, the main anti-hero were the *Zamindars* (landlords), who oppressed the hapless peasants and deliberately made their lives more miserable. There was significant remorse and disdain pertaining to the cruel caste system, and political apathy was showcased in the movies of this time period. It must be understood that in the period until the year 1970-75, movies were extremely depressing and sacrifice was the main theme.

Post the 1975-85 decade, India cinema created a new anti-hero in drug-mafias and black marketeers. This was the time when the malpractices due to the License Raj were at their peak and a fringe of wealthy people (flaunting their expensive Japanese-made cars and Swiss-made watches) exploited the poor and the hapless Indian. In general, this was an age of realism, with films demonstrating the triumph of morality over evil. Between 1985 and 1995, Bollywood films incorporated topics that were relatively strange to the typically conservative Indian culture. There was sex, drugs, drama, extra-marital affairs and unfaithfulness and according to most film critics it was an era of confusion and hooliganism, yet also one of extreme evolution. Representing an evolving India Collective, the Bollywood movies of the decade showcased a central theme pertaining to aspiration, growth and Westernisation. Villains (anti-hero) also changed as now the Indian masses figured out that the real villain is not someone from the general public, but those in the political corridors. Politicians thus became the new faces of evil in Bollywood movies. In the decade and a half after 1995, a liberated Bollywood produced an eclectic mix of movies with themes as diverse as mafia in eastern Indian small towns, corporate frauds in glass buildings in modern Indian metropolises to aliens from outer space. Thus, the contemporary era is one in which Indian cinema has fully arrived, garnering international acclaim. There is a sense of liberation in the Indian film industry now, because social taboos and shame no longer exist. Thus, no subject is left outside the purview of cinema. Evolution of the Indian Collective is thus seen in the way Bollywood movies have changed. Indian psyche has come a long way from the 1967 hit *Upkar*, where the main protagonist was selfless and praised the sterile lifestyle of subsistence provided by an agrarian Indian economy. Today's Indian psyche revolves around aspiration, money, greed and success and altruism is a concept of the past much like the theme in Madhur Bhandarkar's 2006 hit film *Corporate*. To understand today's India and the concept of 'aspiration'; we can analyse the success story and plot of the 2011 blockbuster,

Bodyguard. The Salman Khan starrer became one of the highest grossing Bollywood movies of all time, raking in close to $50 million (Rs. 240 crore approximately) at the box office. The film's storyline/plot is quite straightforward and self-explanatory: the hero falls in love with a girl, tries to communicate his feelings to her, and finally gets the girl after a break. There was nothing grand about the concept yet it baffles many critics as to why the movie went on to earn so much money and broke all records, what exactly was the average movie goer thinking? The answer was straightforward: the average Indian moviegoer is an aspiring bunch who enjoy movies that allow them to live out their own hopes and dreams. When an ordinary Bodyguard has the audacity to fall in love with (even if unintentionally) and even aspires to marry the daughter of his *Malik* (wealthy boss), there is an instant connection because the aspiration is in unchartered territory. There are millions of ambitious drivers, *autowallahs, chaiwallas*, guards, domestic helps out there in India who aspire to do something audacious, which a Salman Khan could pull off in the movie. Such movies, give the lower middle class Indian a window of opportunity to live a dream or at the very least aspire to accomplish one. Therefore, not out of sync, here I might add the evolved form of India Collective, which had earlier assimilated the Western liberal thought (discussed in the last chapter) during the European conquests of India and therefore not surprisingly we now see the concept of aspiration resurfacing in the twenty-first -century 'Capitalist' India.

That the *Bodyguard* of the film eventually becomes rich and can stand tall in front of his *Malik* and ask for his daughter's hand in marriage—this is aspiration, and there have to be means to achieve these aspirations, which is where economics comes into play. If there is no growth, the people in the lower socio-economic strata have no opportunity or even aspiration to grow and this destroys public sentiment beyond repair. However, underneath this very individualistic 'aspiration', there appears to be a deep-seated dissatisfaction with the way India is administered, which is evident in all social strata of contemporary Indian society. As previously stated, there is a sense of despair, doom, and occasionally anxiety as we watch our beloved country perilously sink toward mediocrity. This unease has resulted in a shift in the stereotypical villain of twenty-first-century India—non-cooperation and apathy.

Personally, I am a diehard fan of Farhan and Zoya Akhtar's modern and minimalistic style of film making, primarily because I can associate myself with their movies. However, for the sake of this book, my legions are with Ashutosh Gowariker for his masterpieces, *Lagaan* (2001) and *Swades* (2004). When one watches the movies, it becomes clear that the villain in both cases is non-cooperation among the community and vanquishing of the villain comes through collective action and self-sufficiency (Swaraj?!). Isn't that consistent with our current perspectives? I'm curious as how the new villain in town portends the good things and a new-found rationality.

"It seems that in India everybody is somebody but nobody just an Indian!"

—A foreigner friend

The Social Side of Things

If you read the profile of any American star, politician or any other well-known personality, you will almost always find a short analysis of his/her lineage. As it turns out, a seemingly 'normal' looking American almost always has an English/Spanish/German/Irish/Italian/Scottish/Swedish/Russian or African genetic lineage. Apparently, America, much like India, never was a country with a homogeneous society; it embodies a multicultural, multilingual system. Interestingly, despite the obviously common genetic origins being proudly mentioned in biographies, strangely nobody really takes that stuff seriously in America. America has benefited enormously from the 'I don't care where you originate from' mentality; the country has developed into the world's 'brain magnate' as a result. You may be anything you want to be in America, regardless of your origins; America is not known as the land of opportunity for nothing. I think, if you look at the Indian model of existence (live and let live), it is remarkably similar to that of America. Caste-based system and scepticism towards newer ways still exist but the xenophobia is slowly dying down. Diverse Indian communities are not only living with the natives in several Indian large cities but also B and C towns, where seemingly cosmopolitan diaspora has never been a brand new phenomenon. Due to poor infrastructure and a lack of mutual cultural affinity, earlier Indians from different parts generally refrained from venturing out of their respective regions. However, things changed in a big way during the era of decentralisation when public companies and government agencies brought about a massive demographic reshuffle. Initially, as people moved from one region to another, they used their peculiar cultural affinities as a differentiating marker, but their children (born away from their native place) couldn't care less about these cultural divisions. In his speech 'The Idea of India,' Shashi Tharoor, a former Union Minister of State and renowned diplomat, discusses his twin boys, who, despite being associated with several sub-Indian cultures, identify only with India as their identity rather than having an affinity to a particular region. Vastly true, in Europe and America, immigrant Indians, for example, try to maintain their Indian values but their children find it difficult to identify with a culture they no longer have an affinity with; a Bobby Jindal someone?! One liner, such as 'American born confused Desi', can be directly applied to the children of Indian intraregional migrants as well. It so happens that after a few generations, the progeny of migrants no longer identify themselves to a particular culture but to a larger concept, that of India as a whole. This is Collectivity of modern India and we are moving in the direction, where America is presently found to be a proud example. Not surprisingly, today Hyderabad has a large Sindhi diaspora; Delhi has a large Tamil population and Chennai has vibrant Rajasthani Marwari and Punjabi Sikh Communities.

The growing intermingling of diverse Indian communities into a larger Collective is the beginning of the grand scheme of things. I can't help but recall an advertisement from my childhood. In a national integration advertisement campaign of the 1990s, a wrestler tries to break a stick (and succeeds again and every time) but fails when all sticks are bound together as a bunch. The campaign is significant in giving out the message to all Indians that we will fail if we act as individuals (affiliated to specific religions and cultures) behaving like quarrelling children. Fortunately, the campaign was successful, and contemporary India swears by India's coherence because it understands that the country's different people are intrinsically linked to a single collective, The India Collective. The Indian information technology and the larger decentralised industries in general have played a major role in this assimilation and labour movement.

Taking all this at face value, because of intraregional influx, today's India however appears to have become a repertoire of a number of self-contained communities that have become self-gratifying rather than assimilative. The result has been the present coalition and self- interest groups in modern Indian politics.

Several analysts blamed the economic disparities and slow-moving reforms in the country on the 'Communitism' prevalent in India. Interestingly, upon closer examination, this 'Communitism' is the bedrock of the India Collective, as it enriches it through uniqueness. Every day, fresh stimuli are incorporated into the greater Indian way of life, and India as we know it is constantly evolving into a homogeneous central belief system/hybrid value system, without us knowing.

Playing on USPs

Apparently, there is a long process that has led us Indians to become who we are at this point in time. American scientist Francis Collins, once famously said, "All humans are one big family" findings of his global genome study, which indicated a surprising degree of similarity among all people, and there appears to be no debate over his assertions. If Collins had to choose one country that most exemplifies his insight, India most definitely will be the chosen one.

If you look closely, there is no country in the world which has such immense sense of familial ties than India—in which country of the world are older people referred to with familial references? Perhaps it is India where a random stranger is addressed either as an 'Uncle' or an 'Aunty'. It is indeed strange or might I say peculiar that our collective is so strong that we refer to others instinctively as family. I think this sense of belonging and the affinity with the concept of 'all in the family' has been largely associated with our group activities from dances, to music to watching television. Just as the Gujarati Garba dance is a wonderful illustration of the India Collective in action, I believe that the Mahabharata and Ramayana televised epics drew people together and brought about collectivity in a whole new dimension. I believe that Ramayana and Mahabharata were not only fascinating accounts of our ancestors, but also saved India at a period when the Indian state was in complete disbelief.

The picturised Indian epics reinvented the India Collective and strengthened a sense of belonging among Indians—irrespective of religion, caste, race or creed. As we watched television together, we were merely doing what we are supposed to do as a collective. Therefore in this country, unlike America, there is an 'I really do care where you are from' mentality doing the rounds but that is augmented in equal measure by 'I strangely do have an affinity with you.'

Yet another epoch in modern India is the Atal Bihari Vajpayee and L.K. Advani-led National Democratic Alliance's (NDA) Golden Quadrilateral Road Project, which was precisely a move towards sustaining this very collective through better connectivity and eventual complete integration. Indeed, the relevance of the Golden Quadrilateral concept occurred to me when speaking with an American acquaintance who claimed that post-Independence India had survived this long due to its lack of connectedness. According to him, as Independence's excitement subsided, the new India began to disintegrate as separate provinces developed into self-contained islands of unique cultures and faiths. Due to their lack of connectedness, all these islands remained largely isolated and had very little to do with national affairs. Even though intraregional migration existed, it was miniscule enough to not perturb provincial systems and this was slowly leading to apathy. Today, however, in an age of information and global exchange, this apathy may have resulted in non-association with India as a country, which may have been a major problem to deal with if not checked. The massive connectivity brought about by this ingenious road network worked in the same way as televised epics such as Ramayana and Mahabharata had managed earlier in continuation to what the Indian Railways had achieved.

"An Army man's/woman's behaviour is Bhadra- i.e. Kalyan, Kaarak, Guna & Karma."

—Anonymous

The Defence Side of Things

When discussing the critical role of connectivity in India's Collectivity, it's necessary to discuss the recent India–China skirmish in the Himalayan peaks. In essence, improved connectivity has been a source of conflict between the two nuclear powers with China accusing India for building infrastructure in disputed territories along the McMahon Line. India, on the other hand, has been forever harping on China's massive buildup in the Tibet autonomous region, based upon better rail and road connectivity. This connectivity then is the basis of military buildup on short notices, and both India and China know it well that without such infrastructure, it is impossible to manage troop movements through their massive territories. But the question is, whether this issue only concerns itself with external matters. Speaking of which, the recent disputed news of two Indian armoured and infantry units from Hisar (Haryana) and Mathura (Uttar Pradesh) moving towards Delhi, spooked India's legislative quarters. A military coup has never been attempted in India, and the rumour was eventually debunked; however, it was reported that traffic was purportedly halted to'restrict' movement at the Government's request. Again, we're discussing connectivity!

During a long train journey between Delhi and Pune, I once managed to chat up with an interesting high-ranking military officer and he turned out to be extremely prolific when exposed to my inherent opinion seeking nature. According to him, connectivity (or logistics) has been poor all along but that according to analysts did more good than bad for India. He appeared to disagree with these analysts, who so casually point out that the Indian military could never launch a coup due to a lack of logistical connectedness across India's territories. Lack of proper connectivity somehow never gave independent command centres the confidence to take decisions independently and this 'silo approach' helped at least the internal situations. On the contrary, being an insider, he was of the view that the Indian military never staged a coup in India not because of a lack of connectivity, but due to a lack of intent. The Hindu concept of 'dharma' (uphold and perform entrusted duties) is so ingrained in the Indian military services that leaders take their jobs seriously rather than harbouring underlying megalomaniac ambitions. It's not without reason that as a modern sovereign state, India has emerged as a self-contained nation that is never the aggressor. The positioning of the Indian Armed Forces, which leans towards interception (defensive) rather than aggression (offensive), is based on the fact that there are no points to be proven among the top military brass. It is not without reason that despite the fact that the ancient noble land of 'Bharat Varsha' and its territories spanned from Persian borders in the West to much of South East Asia in the East, India never claimed any territory that is not part of the modern Indian statehood; strangely, unlike China. Today, even with the world's third most powerful military force at its command, a functional nuclear triad capability and space-based assets combined with plenty of foreign currency reserves to wage a long-lasting war, India as a modern nation never threatened any country because the India Collective is all about the country being a Convergent Society. With such capabilities, if it had been another country, the modalities in a certain region would have been hostile. Whether Utopia or not, this convergence is the secret to our collectivity because deep down we all are following the set path leading to *dharma* and its attainment at all costs. This individual sense of purpose connects us into a nexus that may not appear on first instance.

India's 1961 admission to the Non Alignment Movement (NAM) is perhaps the defining moment of India's military doctrine and has structured India's foreign policy accordingly. The basic guidelines of NAM are perfectly in line with the values of modern India and perhaps the '*dharma*' doctrine—non-intervention in other's affairs, cooperation with partners and respect for territorial integrity of other nations. Interestingly, the term Non-Alignment Movement was coined by none other than an Indian, the diplomat VKK Menon during his 1953 speech at the UN. There is a certain profound similarity of this way of thinking to the established Indian ethos.

Historically, India has been following all the principles incorporated into NAM later and there appears a genuine need on India's part to somehow tell the world what it stands for in terms of its values. The NAM is a reflection of Indian principles, as India has practised non-alignment long before it was officially preached. Indeed, India has assimilated aggressors into its collective and reaped the benefits of innovative modes of thought. Militarily, these beliefs have persisted and so impacted our foreign and defence policies.

On a softer paradigm of the geopolitical relationships, India has stayed strong in its commitment to the principles it has upheld for centuries. International aid and modern India's widely publicised stature as a development aid donor is a case in point. With the establishment of its official aid agency, Development Partnership Administration (DPA) under the aegis of the Ministry of External Affairs, India has come a long way from being dependent on global aid to a provider of not only aid but cooperation. Even in the times of the American PL480 aid, when India was one of the world's largest recipients of the international aid itself, the country never used that as an excuse to avoid assisting other less fortunate partners. As early as the 1950s, India started its aid programme by establishing India Aid Mission in Nepal and focused on Cooperation with Partnership and not conditionality-based tied aid. Today, still being a re-developing country, India does not shy away from its obligations and gives out aid in the billions every year, sometimes even higher than several of OECD's [23] Development Aid Committee (DAC) members. And it was not just money that India gave out; in the 1950s and 1960s, India's famed teacher programme for Africa deployed thousands of Indian elementary and secondary school teachers to teach an entire generation of the continent's progeny, who went on to lead a twenty-first-century Africa that is growing in double digits. Entrenched in the values of *dharma,* India used whatever it had to help others even when it had little or sometimes nothing for its own people.

In a 2012/13 survey poll in Afghanistan, India emerged as the most popular country among its peers, hands down, despite the fact that its development aid to Afghanistan was significantly less than that of wealthier partners such as the US—for the simple reason that India as a partner almost 'never intervened in the country's internal matters' and was always a great friend, a co-operator.

The Real Economic Side of Things

"Vasudhaiva Kutumbakam"

As a country and as a Value System, India has been based upon the concept of '*Vasudhaiva Kutumbakam*' and that forms the core from which the context of 'cooperation' is derived. While coming from the social side of Indian society, it becomes lucidly clear that this country has always believed in its ability to imbibe newer concepts and beliefs into its fold infinitely for thousands of years and took pride in its ability to make people cooperate in almost everything. The Sanskrit concept is sublime in a way that it explains what India actually means in one succinct sentence—'The world is one big family' with all its differences: might not be difficult to imagine the magnanimity of a civilisation, which talked about global unity thousands of years before the modern concepts of globalisation actually emerged.

Interestingly, the citizens of India did not only preach this message but imbibed it unconsciously only to face it again in the early twentieth century and that too from the very country they were willing to distance themselves from and whom they blamed for the destruction of Swaraj, England. In nineteenth-century Britain, the Industrial Revolution had spawned a brand new alternative in the name of Social Cooperative movement and India Collective's exposure meant that the concept was incorporated into the core of its belief of cooperation.

Even though, India of today boasts of some of the largest corporate giants in the field of chemicals and pharmaceuticals, information technology, automobiles and machinery, in order to get an all-encompassing perspective, we must consider the real origins of India's true socio-economic modernisation through seemingly inherent collective actions. On March 12, 1930, when Mahatma Gandhi began his 24-day trip to Dandi in coastal Gujarat, mobilising over 70,000 people along the way; eventually, the entire nation stood behind him in solidarity. The Mahatma was on a mission to mobilise Indian people against the exorbitant taxes that the British had levied on salt through their infamous 'Salt Law.' Despite being indigenous, the product was heavily taxed and became a major source of revenue for the British Government. As part of his Civil Disobedience struggle based on non-violence, the Mahatma's Dandi March allowed Indians to understand the power of their collective. The success of the March led people refusing to recognise the British as the controllers of Indian salt (and several other things), and as a sign of protest. No matter how insignificant the exercise might appear today—at that point in time, there was a significant awakening of the India Collective, and salt was no longer a commodity that was at the mercy of a foreign power.

Actually the Dandi March had a prelude 23 years prior—somewhere in eastern India. After a long struggle to find the right spot for his steel plant, Indian industrialist Jamsetji Tata was looking to fund the mega project. Even though, Tata was one of India's most respected brands and enjoyed tremendous good will in India, the sheer size of the capital requirement was beyond the market capabilities. The sum of Rupees 23,175,000 was a colossal amount never seen by the nascent Indian capital markets of the time. Initially, there was a lull and a sense of uneasiness, but it was a period of Swadeshi Movement (Tata Steel website), a critical component of the Civil Disobedience fight in which Indians collectively resolved to replace Indian-made items for European-made goods. There was a great sense of belonging among Indian people and they were showcasing their combined nationalistic pride through consuming only Indian made goods and services. During these exciting times, there was a constant insecurity among the Indian elite that the country was in a way trailing the world in terms of modern industry.

As Europe was in a process of developing its resources and was taking millions of people out of absolute poverty, it was clear that industrial revolution of sorts was not just a Western concept but a necessity for long-term sustainability. Steel as a matter of fact was the backbone of any industrial activity and India was dependent on Britain and America for it. The early twentieth century was also a time when World War I was looming and international demand for steel was extremely high, making the availability of steel in India difficult and with prices often reaching ridiculous levels. According to Tata Steel sources, Tata did not want to raise any money from the international markets because that would have resulted in ceding ownership to foreigners, which would have defeated the purpose of having a homegrown steel producer. As the news reached the Indian people, there was an expression of tremendous support from people from all walks of life.

> *"For the first time in the financial history of the country, the Indian people—the masses, the affluent and even the Maharajas—joined hands to put up the first truly Indian enterprise"* [8]
>
> —Tata Steel 100 (1907-2007) Heritage webpage

Finally, funds in the form of equity were raised from the market, with Jamsetji Tata contributing 11 percent of the total. What resulted from this huge Swadeshi movement was not just an industrial powerhouse that swiftly became one of the world's largest steel makers, but also a movement that permanently changed the socioeconomic structures of its location for the better. Today, Tata Steel is the world's 12th largest multinational steel maker and its mother factory in Jharkhand is built as a feeder and progenitor of one of India's most prosperous cities—Jamshedpur.

From that point on, India began its industrialisation journey; more specifically, following independence in 1947, the country developed its own peculiar systems of socio-economic coherences. As India's industrialisation was largely based around self-reliance, these coherences were based on the principles of Social Democracy, which talks about Freedom, Justice and Solidarity *(Social Democracy Reader 1 by Tobias Gombert)* for Indian citizens and their forbears. In order to achieve these goals of the new India, the Government typically played a very important role of getting people together and working towards prosperity; as mentioned earlier in this chapter (The Fiscal Side of Things), the emergence of the Public Sector Units (PSUs) is a case in point.

These government-owned mega entities were not only economic instruments of India's destiny but repertoire zones of the Indian people. During the early days of the PSUs' establishment, substantial interregional migration of labour, initially white-coloured and then blue-coloured, occurred. That perhaps also brought about a system to inculcate further collaboration among Indian people from all walks of life. In addition to the several industries in India which have been developed through the capitalist function of sole proprietorships/ partnerships, the best part has to do with cooperative movements, which have spawned some of the best known Indian hallmarks of the last century.

It was just another day in March 1959, when seven women from Mumbai explored their grand idea of mass manufacturing *papad* and competing with the best in the market. With a meagre seed capital of Rs. 80, these women set out to accomplish the unthinkable from the identical residential building where they also lived. The entrepreneurs were so successful that within three years, their production had outgrown its premise, the terrace of the founding women's residential building. The project was doing so well, that by 1961, close to 200 women were sub-contracted to make *papads* at their homes and bring the produce for packaging. In 1966, the project was finally registered becoming *Shri Mahila Udyog Griha Udyog Lijjat Papad*, widely heralded as the most promising cooperative movements of all time. The exponential growth virtually guaranteed the cooperative movement developing a solid goodwill in the Indian market and soon overseas. Product diversification was welcomed and expansion called for more women joining year on year. With over 81 Branches, 27 Divisions and a turnover of close to $100 million, this all-women cooperative today provides a livelihood to over 50,000 across India not as employees but partners in success and failure—the secret formula of the movement's achievement.

Not needing an introduction, the Dabbawala System is perhaps one of India's best known business secrets (if I may say so?!). In an attempt to organise informal tiffin suppliers in one of the world's most densely populated cities, two Mumbaikars founded the service of distributing tiffins (lunch boxes) in 1890. The initiative, which was one of the first examples of collectivisation, was initially unionised informally and afterwards through the establishment of a trust known as the Nutan Mumbai Tiffin Box Supplier Trust. The trust's commercial entity, *Mumbai Tiffin Box Suppliers Association* came into existence in 1968. Today, the association's close to 5000 members transit 200,000 tiffin boxes every day across the city of Mumbai without a glitch. These Association Members, popularly known as Dabbawalas, enjoy a fixed monthly salary and staunchly adhere to the trade's rules and regulations. Despite the fact that the members, who often have no formal education, virtually depend on a complex system of colour coding, blunders in the form of wrong recipients are extremely rare. The secret of their success lies in their collective action and cooperation with each other; without such an approach, they could never have succeeded.

In their ground-breaking book, Target 3 Billion, A.P.J. Abdul Kalam and Srijan Pal Singh discuss the example of collective empowerment of the Magar people. In the year 1982, a movement for self-actualisation was about to begin in the Pune district of India's Maharashtra state. Fearing the Urban Land Ceiling Act, 120 families of the Magar community collaborated to form a collective that saw the pooling of over 400 acres of land. Since, the land holdings were not homogeneously distributed, the original land owners formed a company that had ownership equity based on original land contributions. Today, the Magarpatta City[9] is one of India's most modern Special Economic Zones (SEZs) with dedicated corridors for information technology firms and other commercial operations as well as all modern residential amenities available anywhere across the world. The coming together of the Magar farmers in not only forming a self-contained township out of their earlier isolated land but also making themselves wealthy through collective action is a resounding success story of collaboration and collective action. Not without reason, the Magarpatta association has been termed as a model of "inclusive development and social capitalism" (Magarpatta official website). Beautifully put, Nobel Prize winning economist and expert on collective action, Elinor Ostrom writes in her book, *Governing the Commons: The Evolution of Institutions for Collective Action,* "What one can observe in the world, however, is that neither the state nor the market is uniformly successful in enabling individuals to sustain long-term, productive use of natural resource systems. Further, communities of individuals have relied on institutions resembling neither the state nor the market to govern some resource systems with reasonable degrees of success over long periods of time."

Saving the most important collective example for the last is intentional as the 'AMUL Model' has revolutionised the way Indians look at themselves as economic entities. Such is its success, that even institutions such as Harvard University and the World Bank have proclaimed the business model as being very effective in the reduction of poverty. Kaira Dairy Union was founded in 1946 by local farmers in Kaira District who desired to be free of the whims of local firms that refused to provide them their legitimate share. Under the guidance of legends such as Sardar Patel and Morarji Desai, the Anand Milk Union Limited (AMUL) was formed in the year 1946 for the supply of milk and milk products to the city of Bombay. As AMUL expanded under the leadership of Dr Verghese Kurien, H.M. Dalaya and Tribhuvandas Patel, other districts soon realised the potential of collective action and formed their own milk cooperatives. Combining the might of all these cooperatives in Gujarat, the Gujarat Cooperative Milk Marketing Federation (GCMMF) was formed in the year 1973 as a collective marketing and representative company of the movement. Such is the success of the AMUL movement that it is the direct progenitor of India's much talked about 'White Revolution' that increased milk production in the country almost four times since inception. Today, the GCMMF represents over 3,000,000 farmers/cattle owners with an annual turnover of close to $7 billion. Moreover, the cooperative boosts Asia's largest milk-handling capacity and daily cash disbursement records. The business model has been replicated across the country and several Indian states have set up such movements with often great success.

Financially, before and after the nationalisation of the Indian banks in the year 1969, India has had a decent run with its cooperative banks, which took care of much of Indian requirements for over a century. Vadodara's Anyonya Cooperative Bank Limited came into existence in 1889 and was India's and one of Asia's earliest examples of non-agricultural cooperative financing. Popularly referred to as Urban Cooperative Banks (UCBs), India is today home to over 2100 such financial institutions (RBI/OP Sharma) spread across the country. Even though there have been failures and capital risk ratios have been high among such institutions, they are envisioned to fill the lacuna for small and medium-sized enterprises financing, currently not addressed by larger commercial banks.

Failures have also resulted from this habit of collective financial belief system among Indians; financial frauds such as West Bengal's infamous chit fund scandal, popularly known as Saradha Group Financial Scandal due to which several people committed suicide have been increasingly prevalent. Here too, fraudsters took advantage of India's collective decision making spirit for their own vested interests. Perhaps, in order to understand such examples of collective action one must study cases present across the larger Indian subcontinent as well—where undoubtedly, the best example of financial collectivity is Bangladesh's revolutionary Grameen Bank. Founded by Mohammad

Yunus in the year 1983, the financial institution is based on the very concept of collaboration and collective action. The bank started with $27 of founder Yunus's own money, which he lent to 42 village women requiring small amounts of capital for a commercial or other casual activity. The serviced population was primarily composed of impoverished landless or casual labourers (mostly women), who lacked the financial means to obtain commercial borrowings at high interest rates—assuming they could convince a banker in the first place.

With the belief that the poor people not only require money but also have the intention to repay it, the movement was further expanded in the hinterlands of Bangladesh. Before its establishment as a Bank formally, the collective movement depended upon several loans from Government banks but soon reached the milestones of 10,000 and 20,000 members in the early 1980s itself. The movement's lending and deposit activities were handled by local communities forming peer groups that came to be known as 'Solidarity Groups' with the idea that lenders and borrowers must understand each other's perspectives and concerns.

As a business model, 'peer pressure' became perhaps the most important operational tool and as a result loan defaults were a bare minimum with NPAs (Non-Performing Assets) less than 5 percent of the total lending. Today as a successful financial institution, Grameen Bank has an annual turnover of close to $14 billion and is owned by 8 million empowered borrowers along with a minority stake of the Bangladeshi Government.

If we examine the Indian information technology revolution, it appears that we will discover remarkable solidarity with collectivity as well. Unlike the Western technology and manufacturing giants, which were largely 'one-man shows,' Indian IT startups that eventually became blue-chips and an identity of a modern India were by all counts a product of collective effort.

As mentioned earlier, in the Nehruvian India where higher education was highly promoted, India by the 1990s became a huge repertoire of young and dynamic technocrats willing to do different things with their lives. Even though these freshly minted engineers often left India in search of greener pastures in the West, some nationalists remained and thought differently, often in radical ways. As they saw around and explored their environment, these radical thinkers desperately wanted a catharsis to vent out their creative energies and were squarely pointing at entrepreneurship. These young entrepreneurs, many of whom were themselves technocrats, quickly saw the potential of India's enormous like-minded technocrats.

Even though there was tremendous energy floating around at the time, a trigger was required, and the entrepreneur spark just did that. The new-age Indian entrepreneurs did not simply start enterprises; they brought together several bright technocrats in an organisational structure, which appeared to be a step in the right direction. Indian IT revolution therefore in essence was a collective action of technocrats working in a cooperative fashion to create wealth for not only themselves but millions of other like-minded professionals. Indian blue-chip companies such as Infosys, Cognizant, Patni Computers (now iGate Patni) and hundreds of others started just by this very logic of cooperative action. Today, India has developed into a hotspot of IT and other technological start-ups, with thousands of young professionals cooperating to make a difference. The pertinent question is this: are we there yet?

"India has to be transformed into a developed nation, a prosperous nation and a healthy nation, with a Value System."

—Dr. A.P.J. Abdul Kalam,
11th President of the Republic of India and
Father of India's Ballistic Missile Programme

What India Should be Doing (Ideally)?

Time taken by India to reach Upper Income Country status (Best Case Scenario)

Year	2015	2020	2030	2036	2057
India Per Capita $ (Nominal)	1,677.1	2,464.2	5,268.8	10,399.7	81,235.6
India Per Capita $ (PPP)	5,093.4	7,312.2	16,083.8	31,746.7	-
World Per Capita $ (Nominal)	11,745.9	15,002.6	22,165.6	29,704.1	82,754.4
World Per Capita $ (PPP)	12,972	16,555.9	24,460.6	32,779.6	-

Source: Author's Estimates

To successfully build upon the past and present, one must realise the true potential of the future. I reckon that believing in positive outcomes is a great confidence builder, especially for a country that is in transition. In order to build a successful country, we need to have confidence in what the future beholds.

What greater indicator of this potential than the rate at which our combined wealth multiplies? Attaining these goals, however, would not be simple, since India will likely need to maintain an average real growth rate of 7-8 percent for the next two decades in order to achieve 'Upper Income' status. In all likelihood, innovation and collectivity will be the only viable options for sustaining two decades of rapid growth.

In the event of the economy's failure to achieve these expansion rates, rampant income inequality will take its toll on the otherwise positive future, nullifying past achievements.

India's Escape Velocity

(Average real rate of GDP Growth = 7-8 percent)

2012 India's Per Capita income was 14.7 percent of the World's average per capita income

2020 India's Nominal Per Capita income is about 16 percent of the World's average Nominal Per Capita Income

2036 India's Per Capita Income (PPP) will breach the threshold of the Upper Income Group

2057 India's Nominal Per Capita Income will breach the threshold of the Upper Income Group

These estimates consider the fact that the Indian population continues to grow at 2 percent on average for the next 20 years and global economy has an average real growth rate of about 3.5 percent.

India needs to now consolidate its achievements by adapting newer ways of thinking that are in line with what it represents. Not a major demand since we Indians adapt as a part of our identity. At the end of the day, we are part of an evolving India Collective...

Ganging Up for Wealth; Ganging Up Gung-Ho Style!

In August 1942, when 121 men of US Marine Corps raided the Makin Islands, amid Imperial Japanese Army's strong resistance—there was a major morale booster consistently inculcated among the men by their commander, Lt Col (then Major) Evans Carlson. 'Gung- Ho' as it was called, quickly became the most used morale booster among US Marine Corps throughout World War II.

Using this motto to instil spirited self-assurance among his men, Carlson succeeded in his invasion of the Makin Island—meeting his ambitions in neutralising the Imperial army's presence in the strategic location and gaining valuable intelligence for further adventures. Carlson defined the origins of his new revolutionary saying as follows:

> *"I was trying to build up the same sort of working spirit I had seen in China where all the soldiers dedicated themselves to one idea and worked together to put that idea over. I told the boys about it again and again. I told them the motto of the Chinese cooperatives, Gung Ho. It means, Work Together-Work in Harmony."*
>
> —Lt Col Evans Carlson, US Marine Corps.

Carlson got a hang of Gung-Ho as a concept during his days as an attaché at the US Embassy in Beijing, China. During those days, the Japanese invasion and occupation of China was at its height and there were several initiatives taken by locals and their international compatriots to safeguard Chinese interests. One such initiative was the much acclaimed 'Gung Ho' Movement, started in the year 1937 by New Zealanders, Rewi Alley, Edger Foster Snow and Helen Foster Snow. So successful was the movement that it spawned over 3,000 cooperatives within 2 years and reorganised itself under the umbrella, the International Committee for the Promotion of Chinese Industrial Cooperatives (ICCIC) in 1939. It was just the beginning and within 8 years of inception, the movement had collected $10 million in capital from friends and compatriots. Facing difficult times during the Chinese People's movement, the movement was lost in oblivion in 1952 but rose as a phoenix 35 years later and reinvigorated Chinese community living for good. According to the ICCIC website, the cornerstone of Gung Ho is defined as:

"ICCIC's mission is to bring benefits and opportunities to communities in need. Telling people what cooperatives are and how they can be used to turn poverty into prosperity underpins much of the ICCIC's work. The ICCIC promotes the idea of cooperative organization through presentations, seminars, courses and publications."

The concept behind the Gung Ho-style cooperative movement is straightforward; any type of service, irrespective of its nature—whether it is fruit/vegetables vending, cattle herding, milk selling, poultry, sanitation services, automotive workshop or feeder labour for construction activities—can be cooperatively organised. Taking lessons for India, since we are a collective, co-operation in our economic activities may not be a big deal since we have always worked together in all spheres of our daily activities. Taking cues, the Planning Commission of India (PC) has been extremely keen on this phenomenon to sweep the Indian economic landscape. For instance, the PC envisions forming women farming cooperatives during the 12th Five Year Plan, which is a move in the right direction for a new India that should be talking about 'Co-operatisation' and not 'Corporatisation.' In a figurative sense, the 'Gung Ho' approach has the potential to liberate Indians living in abject poverty by ushering them into prosperity and sustainable future through collective action. For a modern and prosperous India to become a reality we must envision a future where all men and women work together in a cooperative style business structure reaping the rewards of material wealth and psychological relief.

Thus, the spread of prosperity in a sustainable manner is the ultimate 'thing to do' for the Indian policy makers. It has been proclaimed time and again that in order to harness the much talked about Indian demographic dividend, the country must provide employment (and resultant prosperity) to its young or risk social upheaval. Given the limited time available to effect critical reforms, India must offer possibilities that are both easily accessible and economically conducive. Due to high degree of concentration of economic activity in India, there are large swathes of areas which are currently left outside the preview of development and hence no prosperity creation at the regional level takes place. Hence, the call of the hour is to provide a labour-intensive framework that can be easily consolidated and is readily available; Micro and Small Manufacturing Enterprise (MSME) appears to be the most promising solution. It is the MSMEs that perhaps bring about the 'unassuming' industrialisation that is omnipresent across the country and therefore this sector can be entrusted to provide meaningful employment opportunities to the masses, which would otherwise migrate to already saturated urban centres or languish as the so-called underemployed.

In order to have a future-proof strategy and the nation being globally competitive, spreading prosperity must be the number one priority for India. According to Planning Commission's 'Vision Document 2020', the economy will require approximately 200 million extra employment till 2020 to function successfully. Whatever was achieved of that vision is a different story; the spread of prosperity and the creation of more and better jobs will continue to hinge on the willingness and ability of communities, to invest in "their workers." The current Indian system of labour legislation appears to preclude such long-term labour–employer relationships, hence impeding the development of a body of highly skilled industrial labour and technical staff. Due to the absence of such agreements, required labour skill sets and profit-sharing equations have suffered.

Collectivity through MSME

If we look at the Indian Small and Medium Enterprise (SME) sector, then it is apparent that the sector is the most important component of the Indian economy; the sector is perhaps the best bet for the India Collective towards a sustainable future just because it incorporates what we stand for in the first place. India's SME sector is widely spread and accounts for 80 percent of all industrial organisations in the country. There are close to 26 million* SMEs, which employ 60 million people in India. Also, the highly labour-intensive SME sector contributes 45 percent of all manufacturing output of the economy and 40 percent of the exports. However, there is a dearth of support infrastructure accessible to Indian SMEs, and they encounter numerous obstacles in realising their full potential; this is one of the reasons why the secondary sector is underrepresented in the GDP. Land availability, financing facilities, skilled labour, lack of innovation and support infrastructure are perhaps the biggest issues facing the SME sector today. According to IFC research, both Micro and Medium industries are hugely dependent on debt and are underfunded with only 38 percent of requirements being met. Also, 95 percent of SMEs are unorganised even though they contribute 11 percent of the Indian GDP.

While comparing the state of the nation's critical sector in terms of SME, I could not help but run parallels with the metiers of India's so-called 'self-employed.' All around us, we see these people working independently, with very little outside help. These 'self-employed,' who could be small shop owners or other small business operators, are the backbone of the Indian economy and have tremendous potential to grow at relentless speeds. As pointed out in the case of SME, these self-employed, who are 'individual' business owners seldom get help in any of their business operations and often find themselves in isolated circumstances. If only these entrepreneurs could collaborate and form their collectives. This way they can have access to not just financial services, tutorials (advice), but also to a a safety net (examples of the Marwari Apprenticeship opportunities within fraternity-run businesses).[10] Becoming organised will help small businesses in being part of a lager cooperative company that has more bargaining powers and represents their interests more effectively.

So how can India use its growing SME model into a prosperity-inducing all-engulfing doctrine? Like the Gung Ho cooperative system, Indian communities can organise themselves into enterprises that can sustain the entire nation. When one looks around, it is not difficult to find the growing number of farmer suicides, poor access to education systems and poor financial inclusion capacities across the country. All of these issues of marginalisation appear to be tied to a lack of cohesion among individuals and communities that are incapable of forming collectives for their own good. Imagine a community of farmers, each holding 3 *bighas* of land on an average coming together forming a cooperative that represents their collective interests. Imagine, in a village, 100 such large and small farmers combine their resources, together tilling 300 *bighas* of land—increasing their bargaining power in the market considerably under a cooperative company representing their collective interests.

Think of it as a modern democratic version of the erstwhile *Soviet Union's Farm Collectives* and *Israel's Kibbutzim Clustering*. As envisioned by the Goa Government under Manohar Parrikar, with collective resources, there will be collective financial inclusion with all families banked and having collective access to financial resources such as easy loans and insurance as the cooperative company (operating under the SME umbrella) formed will mitigate the problems of strict 'Know Your Customer' (KYC) mandates of commercial banks. The larger bargaining powers will help these farmers, who will organise themselves into a company setup with a democratic division of labour, to achieve maximum efficiency. When a person is comfortably ensconced in a large self-sufficient community, there can never be a situation of socio-economic loss or insecurity because the community itself will take care of its members; requisite skilling, education and future planning will eventually become a community responsibility rather than depending upon individual prerogative and access.

Also, since more people become organised, they will become banked (already recommended by the *Nachiket Mor Committee on Banking Reforms & Financial Inclusion*, which envisions 100 percent financial inclusion for over 18-year old Indian citizens by January 1, 2016) and thus contribute more to the larger community, both through taxes and increased available capital with commercial banks due to more deposits. The entire problem of marginalisation will be solved through such collective action across the nation.

In this direction, the Indian Government has already initiated several similar projects aimed at utilising collective powers of the community. AAJEEVIKA—National Rural Livelihood Mission (NRLM) operational under the Ministry of Rural Development is a case in point and is now being adapted in all Indian states for maximum inclusion. The NRLM was implemented as per the recommendations of *Prof Radhakrishna Committee on Credit Related Issues* under the earlier less successful SGSY scheme. The following were recommended by the committee to eliminate rural poverty *(NRLM Progress Report 2012-13—Ministry of Rural Development):*

- Mobilising all poor households into functionally effective Self
- Help Groups (SHGs) and their federations.
- Enhancing their access to bank credit and other financial, technical and marketing services.
- Building their capacities and skills for gainful and sustainable livelihoods development.
- Converging various schemes for efficient delivery if social and economic support services are to be given to the poor with optimal results.

With the launch of the Planning Commission's India Backbone Implementation Network (IBIN) that envisions to get Indian industry and service providers in a 'standardised' order through a Japanese style Total Quality Movement (TQM), the SHGs might be organised under NRLM and will be better positioned to gain expert knowledge transfers through regional IBIN teams, and hence remaining up to date with latest requirements and future scenarios. The NRLM programme is in line with India's UN mandated Millennium Development Goals (MDGs) until 2015 and is expected to play a major role in India's post MDG 2015 (SDG) strategy to reduce poverty and create value across the economy.

However, I believe that the NRLM has a restricted vision and is currently focused on rural India's economy, which is both critical and populist. The strategy can be slightly more effective if it considers all facets of the economy, including urban India. Given the high level of marginalisation and vulnerability experienced by rural migrants and small business operators in India's urban milieu, enactment of such a scheme is critical. The government was expected to identify viable vocations for local people to organise themselves under this initiative; for example, the Bihar government has been on the lookout for good concepts that can be employed as models for the local communities.

However, thinking on a higher plane, I believe that since Indians have always worked collectively, there may not be a requirement to have a rural economy only-organisation or a search for suitable métiers. In the larger scheme of things, everything in India can be 'co-operatised' and spread of prosperity can be actuated through collective action. As mentioned earlier, Indians have organised themselves several times historically and often successfully; Gujarat's AMUL milk movement was recently praised by the Harvard community and the World Bank and was considered as a road map for solving India's poverty problems.

Collectivity can even be applied to community living as communities organise and mandate themselves to take care of the municipal operations rather than depending on their overstrained Urban Local Bodies (ULBs). As an example, when it comes to tap water, only 43.5 percent of Indian households have access—with rural India accounting for only 31 percent. Alarmingly, 11.6 percent of India makes do with non-treated water from any source available. Seemingly, problems concerning water can squarely be attributed to poor connectivity (of another sort!) of households in both supply and demand side of the value chain. Census 2011 states that 48.9 percent (63.2 percent rural) of Indian households have no access to any kind of drainage, a system which best transports waste water into sewage plants for treatment and eventually reuse. It is not surprising that the installed capacity of waste water treatment in tier 1 cities is only 32 percent of total sewage produced; the situation in tier 2 cities is even worse with a treatment capacity of only 9 percent. If people join hands and take water management at the micro level through community rain water harvesting and drainage systems, rather than depending on duty-bound ULBs, the health situation in this country could be literally in people's own hands. While much has changed since the launch of the *Swatch Bharat* campaign and the Smart City Initiative, many of the worries remain serious.

Delhi's Aam Aadmi Party famously talks about 'Mohalla Sabhas' that will manage and represent community interests at the very grass-root level, hence effectively removing the over dependence on municipalities and local MLAs. While on the other hand, India's erstwhile Planning Commission (PC) talks about 'village cooperatives and small land problems' in the 12th Plan Document (2) in order to increase cooperation level at the 'gram' level. In his profound work, *Humanizing the Economy: Cooperatives in the Age of Capital*, expert sociologist John Restakis points out, "Cooperatives invite worker-members to invest their identities in their work, to see their work as extensions of themselves through the mechanisms of shared ownership and personal control. Any workplace can undergo a profound change in meaning if it shifts from being primarily a mechanism for the generation of profit over which one has no control, to being a community of relationships with an inherent worth of its own."

Need I say more about the future of the India Collective? Fortunately, we are progressing in the right direction and are merely processing information that represents us in the true sense—it is indeed in our DNA. It's time to Gung Ho and gang up!

"We must learn to live together as brothers, or we will perish together as fools."

—Martin Luther King Jr.

Inculcating the Commonality among the Common Men

The Common Man, by R.K. Laxman

Legendary cartoonist R. K. Laxman's caricature of 'The Common Man' is the most befitting tribute to the argumentative yet intelligent Indian 'common' man. The character is a true representation of a retired lower middle income man who wears the quintessential dhoti and a Western jacket, which is probably a remnant of his *babudom* (government job) background. His age has given him maturity; he owns nothing much and is content with whatever he has in life—importantly however, he wears glasses. If one is to make a correlation between the common man's glasses and babudom past, it is clear that the man is very much aware of his surroundings and is intelligent enough to make his electoral decisions based on his perceptions of the state of affairs. Even though, as represented, this man believes to keep on walking without pondering over the past; he understands where he stands and believes in a better future.

In this entire process of generalising the 'Common Man' however, it seems that the modern Indian common man has become somehow indifferent to his awareness and forgotten what it means to be common. You see, there is nothing insignificant or derogatory about being a 'commoner' and that has been very aptly pointed out by R.K. Laxman; there is more to it! Being common is being a responsible co-owner of a common idea which is shared by all of one's countrymen/women. Common in fact is the 'common' value system that one shares with his/her fellow citizens and that is what makes a country unique. The Principle of Commons, from which the concept of Commoner/Common Man has emerged, actually symbolises the sharing of natural resources, culture and values amongst a society of free people. Modern economics may have played a role in the disconnection between ownership and property, taking the society away from the argument of 'Responsibility' towards 'Rights'. India of today is a classic example of this very disconnect, and there is nothing Socialistic or Capitalistic about it.

In light of the sharing of the common idea, there is a very thin line demarcating 'public owned' and 'common owned' properties, which in real terms are one and the same thing. But apparently, perception is very different from reality. As is the case in several private townships, assets such as parks, children's rooms, and recreational facilities are owned and maintained by the township community and hence become 'common owned'. In the same way, in small rural communities, the village temple, *panchayati chabutara* and the village well are owned and maintained by the village community and hence become 'common owned'.

There is a lot of respect for these assets because the said communities take great pains in taking care of them by paying for their maintenance by willingly digging deep into their shallow pockets. People do so because of peer pressure in the community of which they are part. However, the same people go out of the way to destroy public property in the name of mob fury not realising that the asset that is a victim of their immaturity is nothing less than that common asset they protect so dearly out of peer pressure. A public or government-owned asset is a common asset as well because it is bought and maintained from the hard earned money of the tax-paying community. Sadly, modern Indian common man/woman does not believe that his/her nation's property is in fact his/her property, which he/she shares with his/her community.

Until and unless the common man/woman does not understand and associate himself/herself with the common idea of India, there can never be a successful Indian community. We the common men/women are just not common citizens of India but the beholders of the idea that our country represents as a nation. We must talk about our 'Responsibility' towards our country in the same breath in which we demand our 'Rights'.

> *"Ask not what your country can do for you; ask what you can do for your country."*
>
> —John F. Kennedy, Former US President

The Government scheme of MGNREGA is a great example of the question pertaining to the Rights and Responsibility equation. The scheme that was implemented in the year 2006 is an employment guarantee scheme with a budget of over Rs. 80,000 crore per annum. Nearly 50 million people are said to have benefited from the scheme's scope, and rural income levels have increased remarkably (one of the major reasons of rising food inflation at the CPI level). However, in this mandate one aspect has been clearly overlooked at the local level.

Apparently, as per its implementation policy, the MGNREGA scheme is designed in a way that 60 percent of the budget is reserved for wage payment, which leaves little room for permanent asset creation—the problem however is bigger than this situation. On the ground level, it is clear that rural communities engaged in whatever asset creation that is achieved, do not participate in that created asset's maintenance. Because the community no longer gets paid for it, these assets are conveniently considered as public assets rather than being considered as common assets, and, hence, out of bound for the community's ownership directive. If these assets are created by the community for its own betterment with the help of government money, how come they are not considered so? We all have the answers. In *Target 3 Billion*, Kalam and Singh have discussed in detail how collective action can help India's rural communities in gaining a good quality of life through self-empowerment. While doing their analysis they have also mentioned the times when this does not happen: according to the authors, "The absence of clearly defined long-term incentives, that are sustainable, would eventually lead to an uncontrolled 'run' in the short term, ending in failure over a period of time or over a larger audience."

One argument for the disrespectful behaviour is the lack of local participation in planning and decision making that are done during the time of the scheme implementation at the Panchayat and District levels; however, the answer to the question as to why the community does not take ownership of these assets seriously is generally associated with a lack of peer pressure. As pointed out by Elinor Ostrom, in her ground-breaking book *Governing the Commons: The Evolution of Institutions for Collective Action*, "Because Common Pool Resource (CPR) settings extend over time, and individuals adopt internal norms, it is possible for individuals to utilise contingent strategies, in relating to one another. By 'contingent strategies', I mean a whole class of planned actions that are contingent on conditions in the world."

Not without reason, several renowned NGOs such as PRADAN and FES increasingly talk about the MGNREGA scheme's future as converging with other government schemes dealing with community ownership and cooperation and rightly so. Without doubt, the idea of community and the connected idea of governance through peer pressure is the only way forward and people must organise themselves accordingly. We must point our fingers at ourselves first before we point them at others; only then will we live a dream of an 'India First' rightly propagated by the BJP. The blame game has to stop and the Common Man's most apt description must incorporate 'collective responsibility' as well.

"We are greater than the sum of our individual Ambitions..."

—Barack Obama,
44th President of the United States,
While addressing the American public after being re-elected for a second term

The Pointlessness of Urbanisation

> *"Don't run to the cities, stay in your village—you can live well there too."*
>
> —Anna Hazare, Social Activist, in his August 15, 2011 speech

How much urbanisation can happen in India? Is it really required? From an outsider's point of view, with its cutting-edge and innovative industry, Germany has set benchmarks for the world to follow. It comes to no surprise that Germany today has over 60 multinational corporations operating in some of the most high-tech industries of the world. Strangely however, while living there, I realised that less than 10 percent of these Fortune 100 companies were based in Frankfurt or Munich!

To understand what makes them click and how Germans do what they do without being in big cities, I decided to understand the system from within. I realised that the legendary German attention to detail and sheer perfection comes from local artisans who pride themselves at being the best in a trade. Apparently, business management in Germany appears to be more concerned with a certain town's collective passion for a product and less with high-rise glass buildings in cities: precisely the reason why most German companies are not located in big cities but in the German heartland and are part of the local identity.

Likewise German prized companies such as Volkswagen AG, SAP AG and Adidas are based in German hinterlands and not Frankfurt. Germany therefore does not exist in its cities; it exists in its hinterlands, the home of its prized *Mittelstand* (Mediums-sized companies). On the other hand, apart from being cultural melting pots, large cities in Germany have a well-defined role of only acting as transportation, administrative hubs and financial transaction facilitators of the country.

German Metropolitan Regions

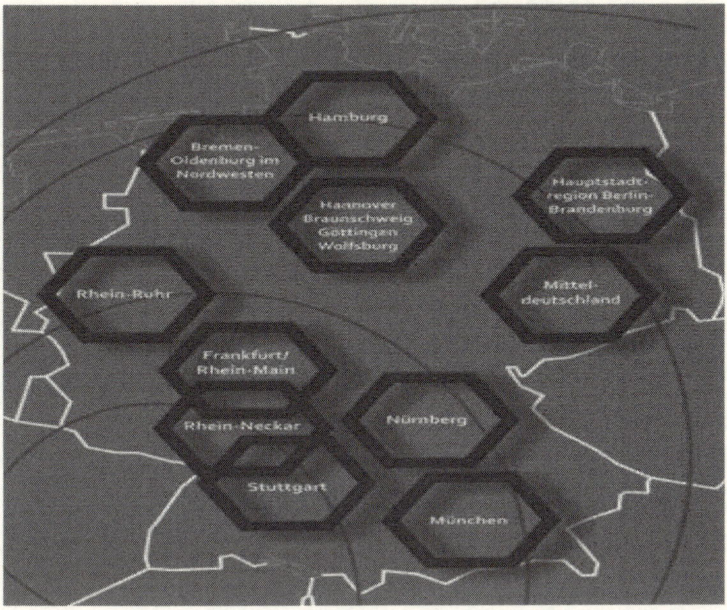

(Source: IKM-Initiativkreis Europaeische Metropolregionen in Deutschland)

Following closely Walter Christaller's Central Place Theory (CPT), the industrial/corporate set ups such as Rhine–Ruhr and Frankfurt–Rhine–Main Metropolitan Regions, offer the German economy the gift of decentralisation and equitable distribution of wealth. To meet these omnipresent employment opportunities for its people, Germany has devised 'Larger Metropolitan Regions' that include large chunks of populations in singular economic zones.

This facilitation allows local people to expect and find employment opportunities in their backyard. As I understand, what this set up does is that it provides for certain economic units to sustain an entire region's livelihood. Little wonder people not only have an employer in the backyard but also a brand to relate with in their day-to-day life. Examples that can help understand the concept include the town of Wolsburg (Hannover-Braunschweig-Gottingen-Wolfsburg Metropolitan Region) that not only matured economically because of Volkswagen AG but identifies itself with the brand. Also, the town of Walldorf (Rhine–Neckar Metropolitan Region) at one time became the wealthiest town in Germany after the establishment of Heidelberg Engineering and SAP AG; the town identifies itself with these high-tech companies.

On the contrary, in India, large cities are the economic sustainers and not mere nodes, while the hinterlands (having no economic sustainability support system) have become a repertoire of the unemployed (or underemployed) struggling for ends to meet. Describing this anomaly, respected Indian sociologist and JNU Professor Dipankar Gupta often talks about his concept of 'The Nowhere to Go Crowd'[11] in his editorials. He says that a class exists in India that serves as a feeder to mass movements or any other anti-social hooliganism.

The reason stated by him is the lack of sustainable skill level among the members of this class that prevents them from having gainful employment. Obviously, if people are meaningfully engaged and have a 'life', they will have no time to get influenced by haranguers and zealots. Even though, smaller B and C grade towns have been exhibiting exuberance and a spurt in consumerism, larger parts of India are still dependent on big towns, which are often very far away and not easily accessible. If you count the top economic centres in a country of 1.3 billion people, there are 51 towns with a population of over 1 million.

Even if these towns can generate enough employment opportunities that can sustain the entire nation, there will still be centralisation of social and economic development—with chunks of the population still finding itself outside the purlieu of development. Increasingly, migrants are finding themselves as being 'Economic Refugees' in larger metropolitan centres such as Mumbai, Chennai and Delhi because of their 'perceived' economic opportunities in a country where they are limited.

Over 1,350 million people share a GDP that is less than half the size of Germany's 85 million people (in nominal terms).Small opportunities, little or no government/private assistance (low HDI index), absolute poverty and a need to travel to distant places for a livelihood leave little room for innovation and logical thinking. The idea is simple: India must adopt the German system of decentralisation and form self-sustainable Metropolitan Regions (on the lines of German Metropolitan Regions) that strategically include large chunks of population.

These Metropolitan Regions will be self-sustained through the establishment of economic units that will be synonymous with that region. I believe that centralisation of wealth and formation of slum clusters are two sides of the same coin. When every region has its own sustainability both economically and socially, residents have a higher chance of achieving equal wealth distribution without having to leave their hometowns, thereby alleviating the problem of overpopulation and excessive stress in established metropolitan areas.

Gujarat's Special Investment Regions (SIR) Model offers effective solutions, but the most stressful problems lie elsewhere in this diverse country—somewhere in the east. Likewise, the eastern states can be industrialised immediately to relieve the burden on the larger centres in the west and north India. It's a known fact that the problem of slum clusters in cities such as Mumbai, Chennai and Delhi is actually caused by poor economic sustainability in the eastern Indian states. Furthermore, the proposed decentralisation will help decongest large cities and will increase the quality of life of local communities.

Rising above the dispute between philosophers and economists as per Jeremy Bentham and Karl Polanyi[12] (in the current context) —the problem of Naxalism (Socialist Movement) engulfing the east and holding the government to ransom is fuelled by unemployed youth of the region who are easily brainwashed by foreign sponsored haranguers. If the communities are given meaningful employment opportunities, the need to indulge in anti-state activities drastically decreases. This happens because then citizens view themselves as responsible contributors to the society and have immediate families to take care of. In contrast unemployed youths targeted by anti-state movements such as Naxalism generally project an image of a hard to resist 'rebel with a gun' (Che Guevara someone?) against the 'perceived' flawed system.

In the case discussed, it is the unemployment scenario and not the social system that gives unemployed youth a justification to take up arms against the Government. Simply put, there has to be a reason to live with dignity and this comes with a dignified livelihood—no prizes for guessing how that is achieved. This is precisely the reason why the Tata Motor plant in Singur (West Bengal) was so important; through backward and forward linkages, it would have created not only the much-needed jobs but also opportunities for local businesses, reduced unemployment levels, reduced need to migrate to other parts of the country (causing slum formations in established centres), raised standards of living and created a more homogeneous society with less inequality levels. The South Korean Steel producer Posco, which is bogged down by illicit regulations in the state of Orissa, is another example. Furthermore, the proposed decentralisation will help decongest large cities and will increase the quality of life of local communities.

I think that Indian industry should be given full leeway to plan and establish (with state-backed checks and balances) employment generation avenues such as large cooperative industrial complexes that are sustainable for large chunks of population (a region's entire community). Innovation should be prioritised because as communities generate additional economic entities via collaborative action, the resulting patentable technologies/services can be used to expand job opportunities (a concept discussed in detail later). Therefore, the best way to uplift people's standards of living, giving them a respectful existence, is to negate the requirement to travel for work and a better life.

The Idea of a New India Not Centred Around Mumbai and Delhi

During the Regional Plan of 2001, the National Capital Region Planning Board (NCRPB) envisioned a method to decongest Delhi

Metropolitan Area from the constant influx of migrants from other less developed parts of the country.

The idea was to have a network of neighbouring towns that could be developed as potential economic alternatives to the National Capital Region. These identified towns, termed as Counter Magnet Areas (CMA) were to be approximately over 250 kilometres away from Delhi and would have a potential to be job creators. For that to become a reality, these towns were to be developed under the aegis of the Ministry of Urban Development, with Asian Development Bank playing an important role. A total of 9 towns were identified as counter magnets and were to be developed to become socioeconomically self-sustained. The towns will essentially provide viable avenues to economic migrants who will be 'kept' away from coming to Delhi instead.

The city of Delhi and the National Capital Region in general, like other primary generators of the Indian GDP, has been a target of economic migrants from around the country for decades, resulting in a near-collapse of the city's social infrastructure and ecological deterioration. a near collapse of the social infrastructure and ecological degradation in the city. Unsolicited migration is regarded to be the primary cause of slum creation, increased crime rates, unemployment/ underemployment, sanitation issues, unsustainable town design, and inadequate healthcare.

According to National Capital Regional Planning Board (NCRPB) data, nearly 23.54 lakh (2.35 million) people migrated to Delhi in the time frame of 1991–2001 alone. The data essentially means that Delhi not only has to create over a million additional jobs but also has to create work and living spaces for an additional 2.3 million people every decade (not considering the population spurt in the existing population). NCRPB has provided a typical description of a migrant to Delhi as following:

- Typical age of migrant is 17 years
- Total literacy of the migrants is 70.18 percent

- Male migrants are 56 percent
- Unskilled or semi-skilled migrants over 40 percent of total
- Savings accounted for 34 percent of total income
- Primary reason for migrating;
    - Finding employment
    - Joining an already migrated family
- Primary Origin Points (OP);
    - Bihar, Uttar Pradesh, Madhya Pradesh, Punjab and Rajasthan

Thus, Delhi serves as a microcosm of the patterned migration-based problems faced by a few economically developed regions of the country. Migrants originate from economically backward areas where lack of economic avenues lead to a lack of employment generation. Large metropolitan areas attract intraregional migrants because of perceived economic opportunities that are not available in origin points (migrant home states). According to estimates[13] India as a country, at any given time has 100 million migrant workers (18 percent daily wage earners) circulating across the country with 30 percent of them being long distance travellers. In fact, 35 percent of urban Indian population is migrant-based, with migrants contributing to 10 percent of Indian GDP.

Since labour movement (induced by migration) is free from any restrictions, there is a lack of fundamental coherence in labour modulation, resulting in permanent unorganisation. As a result of this uninvited labour migration, the market is oversupplied, resulting in lower prevailing wage rates and bargaining strength (a classic example of David Ricardo's *Subsistence Theory of Wage and the Wage Fund Theory*). The condition is further exacerbated by draconian Government regulations that stipulate overprotection for employed (on-roll) workers. Therefore, the chief reason for the problems faced by Indian labour stem from the fact that employers often find it convenient to employ labourers on an 'as and when' requirement basis, virtually providing no dignity of an employment contract. When these two seemingly unconnected issues are combined, they have caused havoc on Indian work conditions (blue-collar level) and on the state of labourers.

As India slowly moves towards a free-market economy system, it is pertinent to first correct the underlying problem of unsolicited intraregional migration and then close loopholes exploited by the market actors.

Several proponents of the great Indian migrant's dream contend that vibrant metropolitan centres are actually centres of refuge providing safe haven to harassed populations belonging to Scheduled Castes and Tribes (SC/ST). In fact, on the contrary, according to data released through Census 2011, slum population in urban India that belongs to SC is only 12.6 percent of the total population: comparing this to the overall SC population, which is 16.6 percent of the Indian population, there is a drastic change in opinion. When the ST population is considered, the disparity becomes much more pronounced, since the ST slum population accounts for barely 3 percent of the entire population, compared to the ST community's 8.6 percent share of the total Indian population.

Even though I do not discount the harassment that the so-called backward classes face in this country, but merely asking them to migrate to protect themselves is not a long-term viable solution. There must be a strategy where people of all 'categories' irrespective of caste and creed are rehabilitated and guaranteed minimal dignity of life. In a country where almost 65 million people live in slums, with no basic sanitation or other services, we definitely need to rethink our strategies to provide these people a dignified quality of life.

Reiterating, one solution could be the German Metropolitan Areas. Before delving into the concept, we must first understand how urban economic systems work in Germany. Apparently, the success of German decentralisation stems from the fact that the country has successfully removed the demarcation between a pure urban and pure rural area. Rather than that (as described above), there are metropolitan areas that oversee an entire region, and this is the type of system that India must embrace. Simply emulating China's model, where forced urbanisation is being promoted by the state through massive fiscal push (valued at over $2 trillion) will definitely not help India's cause. The India Collective's need for collaboration requires harmony in the system, and therefore, I think that an effective way to percolate wealth is to have urban centres expand on their own and take associated rural areas in their collective, eventually diminishing the urban–rural divide.

As a first step, there has to be standardisation in terms of manufacturing/service standards and quality management. The recently unveiled, Indian Backbone Implementation Network (IBIN), which according to the erstwhile Planning Commission would help create such an 'An Ecosystem of Collaborative Action' in India, will be a great development in my opinion. The concept, which was integrated into the 12th Five Year Plan, derives from the fact that India suffers from policy paralysis as a result of a lack of coordination among various departments (public and private); another issue stemming from a lack of cooperation when there is opportunity for it.

The Commission envisages an independent nodal agency, on the lines of Japan's much talked about Total Quality Movement (TQM), which has been credited for making Japan a high quality source of goods and services, creating enormous wealth for that country. The Planning Commission, however, would have wanted the IBIN nodal agency to be independent from the Government and that which 'helps' standardisation rather than 'enforcing' it. This is where I beg to differ.

The Government's Role

I, on the contrary, believe that it is still too early to solve the un-organisation problem through merely dovetailing the industry. Negating the state's role is wishful thinking as India Collective's twentieth century experiment with the Central Government's father-figure stature has been already assimilated and is still pragmatic today. Collaboration and eventual co-operation can come only by the state showing the way and that is precisely what is required. Given IBIN's importance (even though a central coordinating agency is desperately required in India in order to have the mixed model [urban–rural] approach), it must function as a well-oiled government agency accountable only to the Indian judiciary, much like the Election Commission or the Planning Commission/Niti Aayog itself. In my view, if we have a nodal agency that does not have a constitutional backing, the concept will remain a non-starter. No matter how critical we may be of our system, it works and gets things moving. Why can't we have an IBIN-type agency that can act as an 'Enforcer/Implementer' with the Planning Commission/Niti Aayog remaining as a 'Planning' body? While I do not think that the Planning Commission/ Niti Aayog is obsolete, I also don't think that a new enforcer agency will bring about complexity in the system either.

Therefore, for the sake of standardisation and structure, we must overhaul the Indian legislature at the earliest. One possibility is to designate one Metropolitan Region (incorporating urban and rural areas in accordance with CPT theory) in each Indian state, which would be controlled directly by independent committees reporting directly to an IBIN-style body that is part of the Central Legislature. While current state boundary demarcations would likely survive, actual state legislative authority will be limited to periphery state territories outside of the state's respective Metropolitan Regions. Metropolitan Management can be on the lines of Bangalore Political Action Committee (B-PAC), a citizen lobbying group, which uses its collective might and social influence behind a political candidate, whom they trust. Thus, we can have our own version of Germany's Metropolitan Region concept—through what I call Metropolitan Centre Managing Committee (MCMC)—thereby bridging the rural–urban gap and virtually ensuring a collaborative approach. Finally, we want deserving and educated folks to manage the show; why not in this manner?

To explain the concept further, each Metropolitan Region will be autonomous and directly regulated by the Central nodal agency (Centralised Leadership for a Unified Strategy). We must keep in mind that in order to achieve maximum efficiency through decentralisation of industry, we must have maximum centralised leadership for effective co-ordination. There has never been a greater demand than there is today for the development of multiple Metropolitan Centres with independent Managing Committees that transcend state borders and are not subject to frequently inefficient state legislation. In order to hold the Committees governing the Metropolitan Centres responsible, we must envision a Central Commission that will be in direct control. The so-called National Metropolitan Centre Authority (NMCA) (an IBIN evolution albeit in an enforcer avatar), even though independent, will be constitutionally backed by the Government of India. For the sake of our inherent collectivity, the NMCA being a public institution will have appointed tenured technocrat representatives from the Indian Civil Services, academia, civil luminaries, labour unions, social scientists, industrialists and Members of Parliament. Every Metropolitan Centre can be in turn managed by respective MCMCs, which will directly report to the NMCA, New Delhi.

To be clear, I am not advocating for an Indian version of the Chinese Politburo, but I believe that for optimal representation and efficiency, a notion such as the MCMC should also include tenured representatives from the above. Metropolitan Regions in India will bring about the first true Industrial Revolution of the country and therefore each MCMC cannot be left upon the whims and fancies of state legislators. This is because this system has been counterproductive in the past. Without constitutional backing for MCMCs, incompetence and regional centralisation of economic prosperity will result.

The performance of each MCMC will then be directly proportional to the competence of a particular state government, and the capabilities of many MCMCs will differ significantly, negating the objective of establishing these Metropolitan Centres. A centralised control of all MCMCs across India will virtually guarantee decentralisation of economic activity and bring about a uniform accountability and decentralised development. Importantly, innovation and the significance of the University Grant Commission (UGC) must not be underrated and should have more power and discretion, giving it a clear mandate. Along with the idea of NMCA, the UGC should become the principle governing body of the several MCMCs across India.

Vision for the Pan-India Metropolitan Region Network

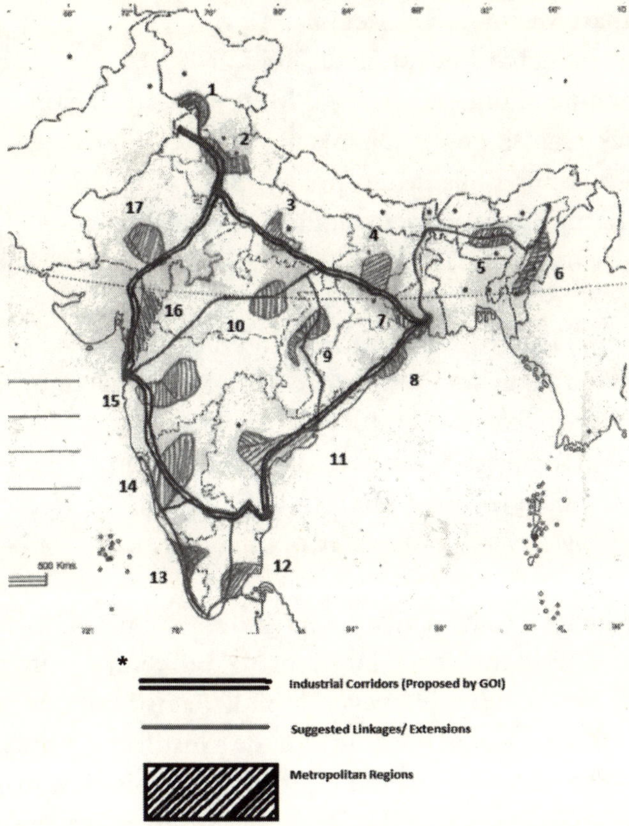

*Suggested by Author

How can the MCMC Network function?

As per the enclosed map, it may be suggested that there could potentially be 17 independent Metropolitan Regions, which can be managed by their respective MCMCs directly reporting to a central NMCA. The regions are as defined:

1. Jammu-Uddhampur Metropolitan Region
2. Patiala-Ludhiana-Ambala-Kalka Metropolitan Region/ Saharanpur-Haridwar-Muzzaffarnagar Metropolitan Region
3. Kanpur-Unnao-Etawah Metropolitan Region

4. Gaya-Barkakana-Dhanbad Metropolitan Region
5. Guwahati Metropolitan Region
6. Dimapur-Silchar Metropolitan Region
7. Jamshedpur-Durgapur-Asansol Metropolitan Region
8. Cuttack Jagatsinghpur-Dhenkanal Metropolitan Region
9. Durg-Bilaspur-Bhilai Metropolitan Region
10. Bina-Katni-Jabalpur Metropolitan Region
11. Vizianagaram-Vishakhapatnam-Secunderabad Metropolitan Region
12. Madurai-Tirucchi-Tuticorin Metropolitan Region
13. Cochin-Ernakulam-Coimbatore Metropolitan Region
14. Mangalore-Dharwad-Hubli Metropolitan Region
15. Pune-Aurangabad-Nasik Metropolitan Region
16. Surat-Vadodara-Anand Metropolitan Region
17. Jodhpur-Marwar-Barmer Metropolitan Region

To facilitate management and connection, it is in these metropolitan regions' best interests to be centred on non-state Capitals or Tier 2 Cities. However, I think that the regions be allowed to transcend state boundaries and include a justifiable number of high and low order sustainers in the regions (an inspiration from Walter Christaller's Central Place Theory). As proposed in this concept, the large district headquarters will function as the high-order centres while district-level smaller towns will form the periphery by being the lower order centres—together constituting a cluster. As development and prosperity percolates into smaller centres, they themselves evolve into higher order centres sustaining other lower order centres in their respective periphery. The concept is quite similar to the current Indian system of graduating small district-level towns to district headquarters as population and economic activity in the centres increase.

Additionally, rather than reinventing the wheel, the network might be built along the lines of the Government of India's proposed 'National Industrial Corridors', which would be modelled after the

Mumbai-Delhi Industrial Corridor. The Government of India has proposed dedicated freight corridors and dedicated industrial zones along these corridors, and I think that the suggested Metropolitan Regions can take utmost advantage of this collective infrastructural might. Together with the dedicated industrial corridors, these respective Metropolitan Regions will collectively build this country into a prosperous and progressive nation that is interconnected and agile—always ready for any eventuality.

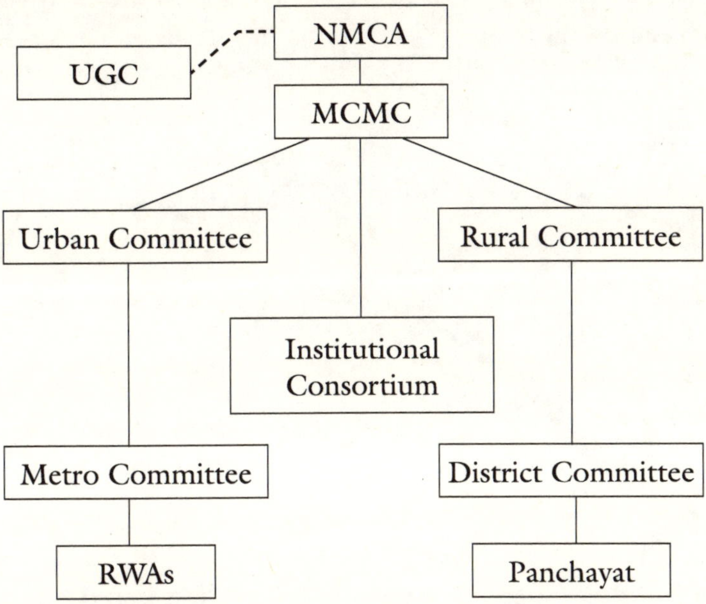

Metropolitan Region Organisational Framework

Example Case Study: Cuttack-Jagatsinghpur-Dhenkanal Metropolitan Region

As a state, Orissa perhaps is a conundrum. Despite being blessed with high concentrations of minerals, coal and other natural resources, the state has remained low income and underdeveloped. The state has been reeling under Naxalism (Left-wing extremism) for quite some time now and has been one of the grounds for hostilities against industry—chiefly being the POSCO crisis (of which I was a hapless spectator as a journalist). It is also a state that exports a large number of regional migrants to other parts of the country due to lower economic avenues at the regional level. Therefore, if there is a state that stands to benefit the most from an ecology created by Metropolitan Regions, it is perhaps Orissa. With abundant natural resources, natural ports and a ready supply of underutilised labour force, there exists a high potential candidate for economic integration though the proposed 'Region under Management' approach. Let's take a closer look at the plan for each region in detail.

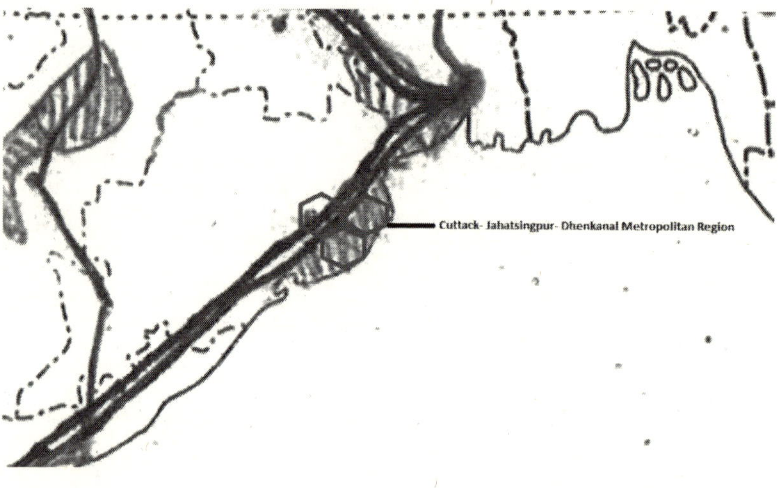

Vision for the 'Cuttack-Jagatsinghpur-Dhenkanal Metropolitan Region

Component Population:

- 2,618,708 (Cuttack District)
- 1,100,000 (Jagatsinghpur District)
- 1,200,000 (Dhenkanal District)

Population under Management:

5 Million (Approx.)

Region under Management

10,204 square km

Economy under Management

- Steel
- Sugar
- Thermal Energy/Coal
- Textiles
- Bidi/Handicrafts
- Ferrous Alloys
- Automotive/Ancillary
- Polyfibres
- Asbestos

Higher Order Centres:

- Cuttack
- Jagatsinghpur
- Dhenkanal

Lower Order Centres:

Example of Cuttack Cluster (Under the K3 Principle of Walter Christaller's Central Place Theory)

Lower Order Centre	Distance from Higher Order Centre (Cuttack)
Chaudwar and Northern Periphery (North)	20-25 km
Mahanga (North East)	30-35 km
Niali (South East)	35-40 km
Banki (South West)	40-45 km
Kantapada (South)	30-35 km
Athagad (North West)	40-45 km

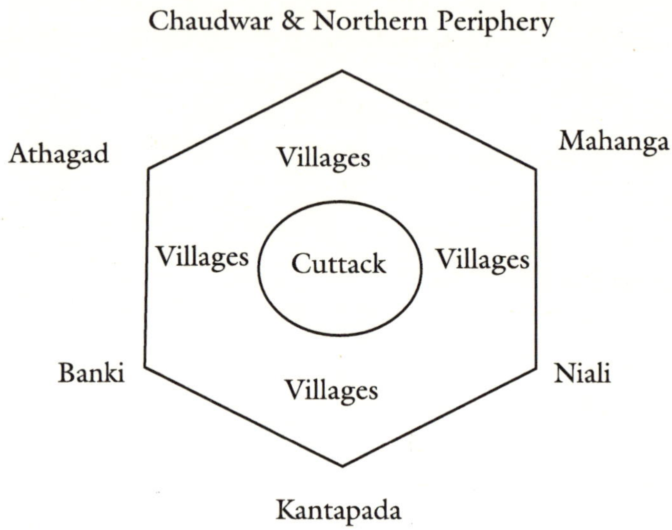

Integrated Cuttack Cluster (one of three clusters in the suggested Metropolitan Region in Orissa)

Based on Christaller's model, which I have modified slightly, I believe it is impractical to assume that lower order centres are equidistant from the higher order centre. However, there can be a related system in place where 'close enough' towns, which are part of the higher order centre's district will effectively, form the periphery. In this case, six towns of Cuttack district namely—Kantapada, Niali, Mahanga, Banki, Athagad and Chaudwar form the lower order centres with the city of Cuttack becoming the core of the cluster and the designated higher order centre. Since, Christaller contends that distances have to be equidistant for ease and ability of travel between lower and higher order centres, it will be in the cluster's best interest to have effective public transport that connects these centres conveniently. By way of definition, the higher order centre offers higher order facilities such as airports, corporate headquarters, multi-speciality hospitals and universities, while lower order centres have basic services sufficient for local residents to live comfortably. According to the Center Place Theory, residents of lower order centres travel to higher order centres whenever they require higher utilities such as specialised treatment or airport services; however, for that to happen they must feel comfortable to access the facilities. For this reason, connectivity is critical in order to maintain a holistic ecosystem free of demand–supply imbalances. The best feature of this ecosystem is that a cluster is comprised not just of urban centres but also of the rural region that surrounds them. A holistic 'Region under Management' approach dismantles the rural–urban divide and represents an entire region, without any distinctions. Individuals are free to travel within the system for work or pleasure while remaining permanent residents of their respective lower order centres, effectively negating unsolicited migration. In this particular example there will be a total three such clusters with three (1*3) higher order and eighteen (6*3) lower order centres, collectively functioning as the Cuttack-Jagatsinghpur- Dhenkanal Metropolitan Region. There will be immense potential that will be unleashed from such an ecosystem, as individuals will be able to find jobs and entertainment centres in their own backyard and will start to associate with their region's specialties.

As explained in the Organisational chart above, each Metropolitan Region will be autonomously managed by the Metropolitan Centre Management Committee (MCMC) that will report directly to the National Metropolitan Centre Authority (NMCA). Since, we are envisioning the dismantling of the urban–rural divide, each respective MCMC will be reported to by an Urban Committee and a Rural Committee, which will in turn be reported to by Metro Committee (Urban) and District Committee (Rural) at the local level. This method will ensure that the same committee (MCMC) will address issues at the urban and rural levels without distinction and with an all-inclusive holistic view. Such a unified command system will excel because the system will spawn 'equalitarian' administrative governance rather than an obsolete system of 'selective intervention' that leads to corruption and mindless populism.

With 17 such ecosystems spread across the country, the country will truly move towards Narendra Modi's often talked about concept of 'Cooperative Federalism'. A system where every region equitably contributes to India's development and helps collectively to build this country into a prosperous and proud nation, whose people work together and innovate to create wealth.

Further Management of the Metropolitan Regions

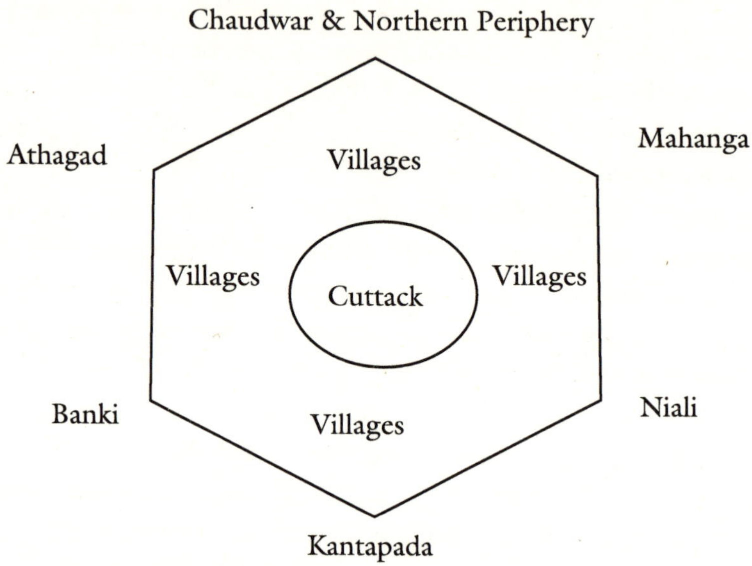

Integrated Cuttack Cluster (one of three clusters in the suggested Metropolitan Region in Orissa)

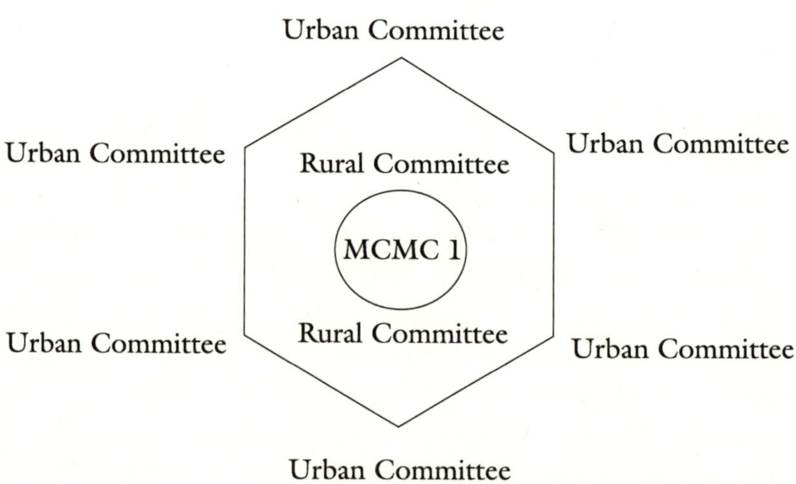

Administrative Centres of the Integrated Cuttack Cluster (one of three clusters in the Metropolitan Region in Orissa)

As far as the administration of the regions is concerned, even though I have discussed the concept in detail previously, I thought that ideally, I should further explain the administrative part of the respective metropolitan regions separately. For the sake of simplicity, I will continue to stick with the Cuttack-Jagatsingpur- Dhenkanal Metropolitan Region, choosing the Cuttack Cluster (1/3). In the Cuttack Integrated Cluster, administrative functions can be holistically divided as per the 'layer system'. The outer layer, which comprises the lower order centres, will be managed as a function of independent Urban Committees. Therefore, in essence, the lower order centers of Chaudwar, Mahanga, Niali, Kantapada, Banki and Athagad will each have an Urban Committee, which will in turn manage the decentralised urban local bodies (ULBs) called Metro Committees. Each Metro Committee will represent at least 50 RWAs; depending upon the number of RWAs in a centre, there will be an even distribution of RWAs among Metro Committees. Collectively, these Metro Committees will report to the single Urban Committee of each centre. The Urban Committee will report directly to the respective MCMC- forming a clear chain of command. Therefore together, there will be several Metro Committees (depending on the number of RWAs) will report into one Urban Committee (representing each lower order centre), which will in turn be answerable to the MCMC. The inner core, which comprises of Cuttack, will function as a component of the Metropolitan Region's MCMC (one of 3 components that make up the primary MCMC) and manage the entire cluster. Think of a Hub and Spoke Model.

The middle layer, which includes the villages between the MCMC core and the lower order centres, will be managed by independent rural committees, each with a population agglomeration of 25,000 people.

Much like district-level village management in the rest of India, each Rural Committee will manage local-level District Committees that will represent population agglomerations of 5,000 each (evenly distributed and depending on the number of Panchayats). Effectively, as mentioned earlier, both Urban Committees and Rural Committees will report directly to the MCMC of each cluster.

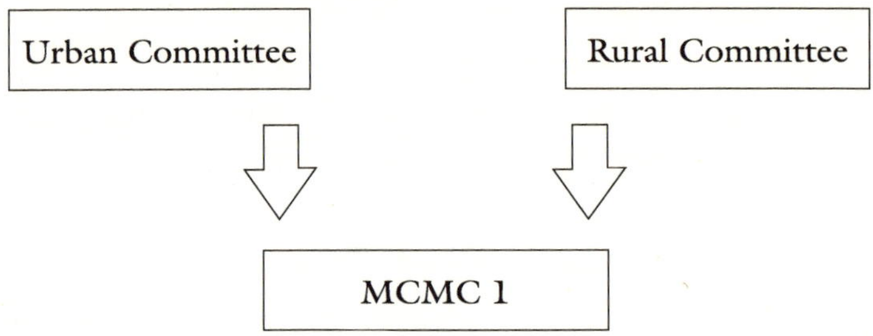

Together, the three clusters of Cuttack-Jagatsingpur-Dhenkanal will form the larger Metropolitan Region in Orissa. All layers of each cluster will be interconnected with high-speed local transportation and world class logistics. There will be free movement of goods, services, capital and labour in the region, and the entire Metropolitan Region (with all three clusters) will act as a single market, guaranteeing maximum ease of doing business and a stress-free lifestyle for residents.

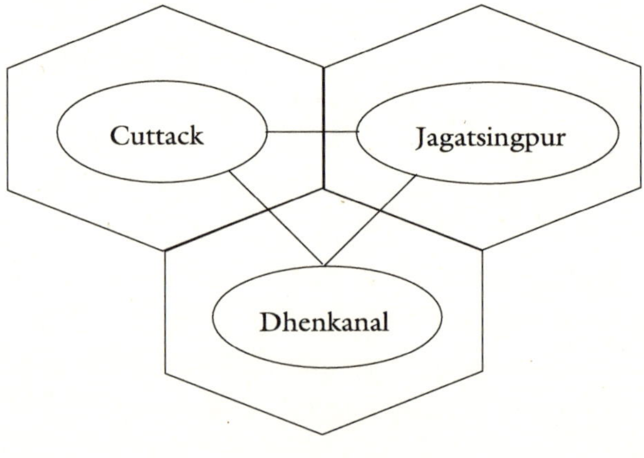

MCMC of the Metropolitan Region

Fostering a Cycle of Innovation

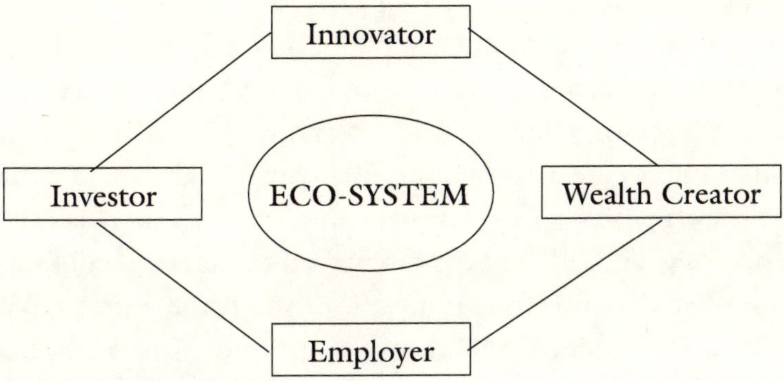

Source: Author's Concept

Economist Joseph Stiglitz an economist, frequently refers to a 'Intellectual Infrastructure' system as being important for boosting incomes through increased productivity.

Without addressing the issue of 'Intelligence Promotion,' there can be no significant wealth development that eliminates inequities. Innovation is not a foreign concept in India because it is embedded in an adaptive value system. We as a nation and as a collective have always been assimilating newer ways of thinking and the best part is that we have always been open to change. Thus, innovation is something that can affect both the way we work and the quality of our lives in subtle ways. In today's globalised economy, innovation is unavoidable, and we will almost certainly need to develop an environment conducive R&D. Therefore for our socio-economic well-being, our strategic defence needs and our foreign policy, we must make scientific innovation part of our modern collective (way of thinking). Currently, India only contributes 3 percent of global R&D spending as per a report from Roland Berger Strategy Consultants. Not surprisingly, the Indian economy's Total Factor Productivity (TFP), or in other words, efficiency of the ecosystem is one of the worst among the newly industrialised nations. Undoubtedly, the best bet for India is to have an Investor-Innovator-Wealth Creator virtuous cycle (setup) that eliminates the need for delineated regional settings and promotes harmony and collaboration. Innovation must result in a system in which the incubated become the incubators of future innovators, cooperating and assisting communities in creating even more riches.

South Korea is a shining example of how innovation can lead to wealth, taking citizens from low income to high-income classification within a matter of a few decades. Narendra Modi's often quoted Korean examples are not frivolous in any way. The country that was able to spawn globally competitive conglomerates such as Hyundai, Kia, Samsung and LG was a country that started building itself into a modern country not until 1953, when the Korean War was concluded. It is indeed remarkable that South Korea advanced its cause within such a short period of time—becoming an OECD member country in less than 50 years of modernising itself. The following tables show the innovation per capita in South Korea and the resultant explosive growth in per capita incomes. The high correlation between innovation per capita and income per capita is drastic. The country started out with peers like Indonesia, Thailand and Malaysia (the so called Asian Tiger Economies) and today leads the way through innovation and collective action.

Such was the situation that even in the 1980s, South Korea was neck-and-neck with its South East Asian economic rivals in terms of per capita income (PPP) but within a span of 20 years, the former 'Hermit Kingdom' was in the so called UN 'high income' bracket, while its peers were stuck in the dreaded 'middle income trap.'

Country	Application/ Population (%)
USA	0.15
China	0.03
Japan	0.28
South Korea	0.34
European Patent Office	0.03
Russia	0.03
Brazil	0.01
India Information Source: WIPO	0.0029

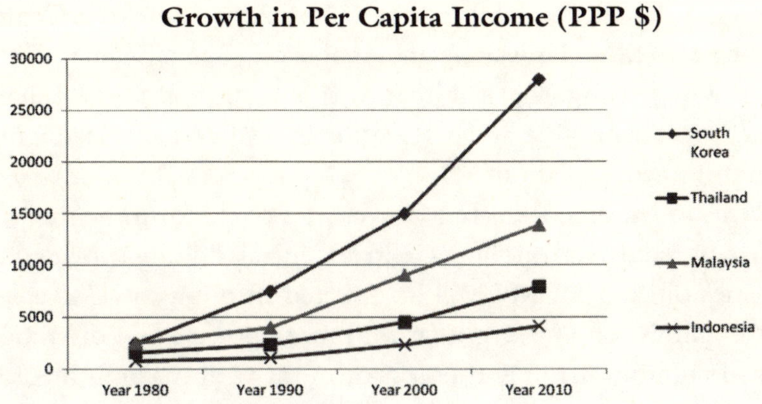

Source: Author's Research

South Korea has hence come a long way from the former President Park Chung Hee's revolutionary *Saemaul (New Village) Movement* in 1970s, under which every South Korean village was given 335 bags of free cement and other building material to self-build infrastructure and become successful under the authoritarian '*Yushin System*'. To a lesser degree, India's central schemes such as MGNREGA must follow this example when it comes to permanent asset creation, but more on that later.

In the Indian Budget 2013-14, the Government of India allocated Rs 100 crore each for 4 'Institutions of Excellence' in an effort to boost India's research-based education; the primary motive or objective was however not clarified. According to the recommendations given by the Naresh Chandra Task Force on National Security, India must establish an Advanced Projects Agency (APA) for conducting 'high risk futuristic military research'. The Task Force has recommended that among others, the University Grants Commission (UGC) Chairman must assist the APA head, who will be the Scientific Advisor (SA) to the Defence Minister. The recommendations emphasise the critical role of university-assisted research and development in India's long-term strategic goals of self-sufficiency. Important examples of such setups include the Jet Propulsion Labs (JPL) at California Institute of Technology

(Caltech) in Pasadena, California or NASA Ames Research Center at Carnegie Mellon University in Pittsburgh, Pennsylvania, USA. There is no denying the fact that without cutting-edge military research, there cannot be any percolation in civil domains leading to meaningful wealth creation.

For this to happen, Research Universities could form the nucleus of each suggested Metropolitan Centre. Central funding provided to universities of each MCMC will be directed through the University Grants Commission (UGC), now with more powers and discretion to provide funding to only those institutions with maximum R&D activity and potential. A ranking-based system, an agenda in the government's mandate (culminating into the NIRF Rankings), for instance can be used by the UGC to base funding decisions. Variables such as patent fillings and Corporate Funding Initiatives can be the key to climb the rankings used by the UGC to grant funding, creating a general competitive environment for gaining maximum funding through maximum R&D.

As with the planned price-controlling rating system for hospitals, rating systems for universities must be developed that assess each university's research competence, published papers (in reputable international journals), and IPRs (patent registrations)—and then rate them appropriately. UGC funding and national rankings will be directly proportional to such ratings. Eventually, Metropolitan Regions must compete for funding and talent. A central body, NMCA in our case, could regulate interregional competition and assign rankings on the basis of performance indicators. These rankings can be used by foreign investors to make investment into a region, R&D partnership agreement with international agencies/universities and funding by the UGC. The National Education Policy (NEP) 2020 furthers the argument pertaining to an innovation eco-system involving educational institutions. How it evolves into something fruitful, is a matter of time.

Progenitors of the Exercise

When Rahul Gandhi speaks at the CII about the requirement of the industry's partnership to build India, he is not wrong when he assumes that Indian corporates hold the key. Furthering my argument, just like the recent CSR mandates, it should be made mandatory for corporate India to pledge a portion of their profits to R&D. Rather than undertaking independent R&D activity, corporate India should establish Endowed Research Chairs at Universities. As an example, Tata Motors, being in Pune can establish the Tata Motors Endowed Chair in Automotive Research at IIT, Mumbai or Bharat Heavy Electricals Limited (BHEL) having a major centre in Haridwar can establish the BHEL Endowed Chair in Electrical Equipment Research at IIT, Roorkee.

Bharti AIRTEL's endowed Chair in Telecommunications at IIT, Delhi, is most definitely the way forward. All companies, whether public or private, having revenues over a certain threshold must be mandated to establish an endowed research chair at any Research Institution of their choice in their respective MCMC. With big corporate money flowing in, R&D will get a fresh impetus with the best minds working to achieve the best results. Brain drain can be effectively controlled as incentive-based innovation becomes the principal component in education and research.

Meanwhile, the sponsoring corporate will reap the benefits of cutting-edge research undertaken at universities. Resultant innovations can further create wealth for the particular MCMC/ Metropolitan Area as innovations translate into industrialisation, which creates more opportunities leading to economic prosperity. We must become a magnet of the world's 'Brains', whether home grown or foreign. A country's ultimate success in today's knowledge-based economy is its ability to attract the best talent, which is also the key to a country's economic might. If tomorrow's innovators are here well before they actually start work on their ideas, the country will become a superpower on all counts.

The Most Innovative and Wealthy Economies: A Comparison to India

Country	Per Capita Income (US$ in PPP)	R&D Spend (% of GDP)	Modernisation & Industrialisation since
USA	54,000	2.70	>150 Years
Germany	40,000	2.30	>150 Years
Israel	35,000	4.20	>40 Years
Sweden	42,000	3.30	>80 Years
Finland	37,000	3.10	>80 Years
South Korea	34,000	3.80	>40 Years
China	10,000	1.80	>50 Years
India	5,100	0.90	>50 Years
Taiwan	40,000	2.30	>50 Years
Japan	37,000	3.70	>100 Years
Source: World Bank/IMF/Author's Research			

Note: The older industrialised nations, such as the United States and Germany, also known as the pioneers, have greater incomes despite smaller R&D spending than some other countries. This is because comparatively newly industrialised nations such as South Korea and Taiwan have been industrialising for a shorter period of time and are in a process of consolidation. Also, latter countries are focused on capital-intensive industry more as compared to the traditional established economies that have diversified and have now outsourced some of their industrial processes.

Social and Economic Structures

The Overbearing Agriculture!

> *"You know something is seriously wrong when we join the Brits and make the weather our favorite topic of conversation."*
>
> —Omar Abdullah, former CM of Jammu and Kashmir State via *Twitter* on the overrated Indian discussions over the effects of monsoon

Even though India is a global leader in information technology and produces the world's largest pool of technology graduates, a portion of the country remains trapped in a time warp. The majority of India is still agrarian and cultivates using the most rudimentary methods. Agriculture is in such bad shape that it cannot be a genuine economy sustainer (citizens cannot depend on it for subsistence). Agriculture cannot be the primary source of employment, as India is certainly not basking in the glory of *Mere Desh Ki Dharti*.

Arcane regulations enacted to promote equality among citizens have wreaked havoc on production over the years, increasing the number of persons per hectare rather than decreasing it. Destroying subsistence, the UP Ceiling Act,* for example, restricts individual farmers to own no more than 18 acres of land, a policy that, far than alleviating inequality, instead diminishes agricultural productivity (Theory of Diminishing Returns). In India, the hereditary division of land has made agriculture so unprofitable that farmers neither have any negotiating/bargaining power nor inclination to innovate production techniques.

With land holdings shrinking and economies of scale not achievable, agriculture has devolved into a source of disguised unemployment at best and is unable to support India economically. Consider the following in detail: Agriculture accounts for only 17 percent of our GDP, but over 60 percent people depend on it for subsistence. This means that agriculture only manages to spread $510 billion among 840 million people, astonishing! If you do the simple math, you will see that in nominal terms, agriculture is able to contribute a meagre $607 per person depending on it for a livelihood. In Rupee terms, factoring the average value of a dollar at Rs. 73, the buying power of a person comes to only about Rs. 44,321 annually (and mind you, it is only the average figure). According to these standards, the majority of citizens who rely on agriculture for a living are on par with or worse off than those who are officially below India's poverty line (earning less than $2 per day), indicating that the majority of

India's 37 percent poorest people have a connection to agriculture. The BPL (Below Poverty Line) calculations suggest that any citizen earning less than $730 a year is living in absolute poverty (cannot afford even two meals a day). The $607 average income provided by agriculture as compared to $730 general BPL income is baffling because theories propounded by Prof. Dandekar and Rath clearly mention a need to have higher calorie intake for people in the rural settings; something that farmers/peasants cannot afford.

With such little income, farmers/peasants not only worry about sustaining themselves but also mounting debts due to volatility in prices of raw materials, pesticides and fertilisers and an erratic Indian monsoon If the suicides of agriculturalists in Maharashtra, Gujarat, Andhra Pradesh, and Karnataka are any indication, agriculture is not a viable sector and India cannot continue to rely on it. Even these modest economic advantages should be examined in light of the fact that they were obtained as a result of a number of technological improvements, high-yielding seeds, and good irrigation facilities backed by the government.

There are very few remaining avenues for increasing agriculture's value per head; even if there is a possibility to do so, the question is, by how much? No country in the world has become wealthy depending on agriculture, why should we be the exception? Why should we depend on it in the first place? For the proponents of self-sufficiency, in order to guarantee our food supplies sustainably, we can have cooperative movements involving large swathes of agricultural land that are managed by a committee of farmers/ landowners.

Whether anybody believes it or not, economics will dictate the future of agriculture and I see it going in the direction of corporate-style agricultural production in an industrial setting. Agriculture has become a capital-intensive industry and today countries that enjoy the highest yields per hectare are not those with the highest ratio of population engaged in agriculture, but surprisingly those that have the lowest ratios. In the United States, for example, only 1.08

million people work in professions related to agriculture while in Australia only 0.4 million people do the same.

In India over 292.8 million (non-co-operative) people are involved in agriculture on the other hand! Talking about the so-called disparities, if you see per head productivity, it is not hard to notice that even with these extremely small labour forces, the United States manages to produce over 60 million tonnes of wheat for its 313 million people while Australia produces 22 million tonnes of wheat for its 22 million people. India on the other hand produces a dismal 81 million tonnes of wheat for its 1400 million people!

Frankly, this is an example of extremely unproductive division of labour and bad human resource management. What's surprising is the fact that we have reached even these dismal levels when wheat production has broken all records; a time when India has had record-high wheat production levels! This is not an example citing a difference in productivity between us and other nations but a difference in smart allocation of labour. From the figures mentioned below, it becomes uncomfortably clear that for a country with high concentration of agriculture-based population, Human Development Index is inversely proportional. This is a global phenomenon; the question is whether we really need so many people depending on agriculture?

For how long can we expect stand-alone farmers/peasants to work day in and day out for very little economic gain so that we can have access to low-cost food grain? One day or the other, people involved will ask for their rightful share and we may find ourselves in a crisis.

Agriculture is already an unpopular profession due to its high labour intensity and low remuneration; migration from rural civilisations to established urban centres is a direct result of agriculture's unsustainable nature. Thus, unorganised agriculture weakens rather than strengthens the Indian Collective rather than strengthening as it gives rise to a conflict between the haves and have-nots. For a collective population with a collective thought process, labour force has to be bifurcated to more lucrative professions in the secondary (industrial) and the tertiary (service) sectors; for those remaining in the primary sector, a cooperative set up has to be the mandate. The concept of 'Kisan Mandi' will free a vast agricultural market to Collective Action ultimately overbearing the cumbersome Agriculture Produce Market Committees (APMC). Moving towards an evolution of *Jai Jawan, Jai Kisan*—Coop is the way!

Comparison between API and HDI

Country	Agricultural Population Index	Human Development Index
USA	0.007	0.9
Germany	0.024	0.9
UK	0.014	0.86
France	0.038	0.88
Italy	0.042	0.87
Japan	0.04	0.9
China	0.039	0.68
Finland	0.045	0.88
Norway	0.029	0.94
Sweden	0.011	0.88
Spain	0.045	0.87
South Korea	0.07	0.89
Canada	0.05	0.9
Brazil	0.2	0.71
Russia	0.1	0.75
Turkey	0.29	0.69
Mexico	0.11	0.77
Australia	0.036	0.93
South Africa	0.09	0.62
India	0.6	0.54

Note: *On a scale of 0-1. The closer the figure is to '1' the higher; closer to '0' is smaller

Source: Author's Research/World Bank/IMF

As per the Economic Census 2005, only about 5.1 percent of the total rural population was engaged in non-agricultural establishments. The following is the distribution of non-agricultural establishments in rural India:

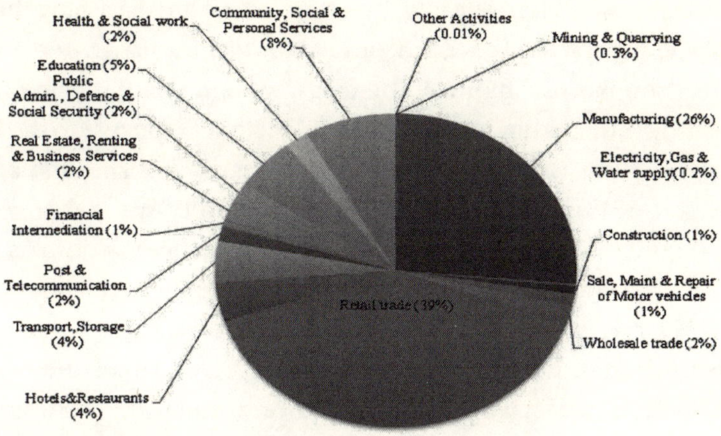

Source: Census 2005

The Argument on Retail Organisation

Today, India is the world's 5th largest economy (in nominal terms) and the 3rd largest economy (in PPP terms), standing tall in a materialistic world that measures progress in terms of a country's actual monetary value. While many individuals discuss the population's per capita consumption capacity, I believe that ultimately what matters is a nation's combined purchasing power..

India, for example, has a per capita income of about $9000 (belonging to the lower middle-income group in Purchasing Power terms) but when you consider the fact that over 1.3 billion people have an average income equal to that, India's combined buying power comes to over $11 trillion, making it the third biggest economic influence in the world economy today. The reason I am discussing the size of the Indian economy is not to inform what India has achieved in such little time from being classified as one of the world's poorest countries but to discuss socio-economic structures that make India. For example, in the 'India special episode' of *BBC Top Gear* (a renowned British sitcom on cars), which was widely criticised for being 'tasteless',[14] an intriguing point was made on Indian business acumen and, of course, the 'shopkeepers'.

Quite true actually, when you consider the fact that these 'mom and pop shops' (often referred by the Western media), have become one of the biggest sources of income for Indians at large. India in fact took the 'shopkeeper' moniker for keeps not because of it being an easy profession/business but because of our collective's exposure to the British way of life. Even Britain has been referred as a 'Shopkeepers' country by the rest of Europe and the topic (protection of small shopkeepers) was a bone of contention during Margret Thatcher's tenure as Prime Minister, vigorously discussed in the Parliament between the Labour and the Conservative Party representatives of those days.

To understand the business model of these small unorganised retailers here, we have to look at these miniature versions of a convenience store as startup businesses that do not really have to expand in operations but just have to continuously sustain themselves. Therefore, modern MBA type concepts such as turnover and margins are simply not considered while drafting a business strategy in this country, as goods are frequently offered at the Maximum Retail Price (MRP). By observing how these enterprises operate, it is evident that there is enormous possibility in retail and that there must be ways to harness this Indian entrepreneurial maelstrom, which has the potential to transform the scope and character of Indian socioeconomic systems.

Organisation of retail is thus the primary concern of today as this can provide the necessary impetus to strengthening and streamlining the Indian retailing for our long-term benefit. Small retailers will continue to exist, as they do across the world, but they must organise to protect their interests and strengthen their negotiating power; it is all about a competitive market (survival of the fittest). As mentioned earlier, the business model of small retailers is different to that followed by large retailers; entry of which will only strengthen the market. Thus, while there would be no genuine competition between small and large merchants, there will undoubtedly be competition between organised and unorganised retailers.

Prior to forming any prejudices, it is necessary to understand the psychology of the consumer. Obviously, the consumer will be loyal to a retail store which offers him/her better value for his/her limited resources. The unorganised retailers will not lose their captive consumer base because the consumers would suddenly flock to large retailers, but because the former will not be able to provide enough value and choice to the consumer. This occurs because a lack of organisation will lack standardisation of practices, and prices are nearly always higher than those supplied by organised retailers. Therefore, there is no question of who will command lower prices and who cannot; it is all about how organised a business really is and that is the key to resilience of any business model.

The concept of cooperative is not new to us Indians, and I see no reason why small retailers cannot organise themselves as business cooperatives and fight the competition effectively. As an example, how many independent milk producers could compete with organised competition prior to the foundation of milk cooperatives in Gujarat and Rajasthan?? Almost negligible! Today, these milk cooperatives have grown so powerful that they have outpaced influential foreign organised retailers at their own game. Lijjat Papad is another example of how organisation helps.

Cooperative movements are the symbols of what Indians can do if they collaborate and get their resources together for a collective good. Cooperative movements have provided a stable source of income for several Indians and liberated them from irregular agricultural yields. According to an article published by businessmapsofIndia.com on July 6, 2011, Rajasthan farmers realise almost 60-70 percent of their consumer price from dairy products alone. Multibrand retailing can also be 'cooperative' by combining multiple independent stores under a single brand (an example is the Sehkari Retailers in Maharashtra). Organisation is, therefore, the inevitability and it makes sense to organise retail beforehand for the sake of a well-managed market, the consumer and the individual retailer instead of pondering over half-baked information. Several consequences of India's retail disorganisation include the following:

- In India, the Consumer Price Index (CPI), a proxy for inflation, climbs faster than the Wholesale Price Index (WPI). This demonstrates why organised retailing is critical for price stabilisation. CPI climbed by 6.93 percent in July 2020, while WPI contracted by (-) 0.58 percent. This is based on the 2011/12 fiscal year. These figures represent variances during the 2020 Covid Pandemic.
- Significant disparities in prices of goods sold by large retailers and small retailers (who sell at MRP) is observed. Large price differentials between specific commodities, such as wheat, oil, and vegetables, are a typical occurrence. Organisation may contribute to inflation by offering more competitive prices. Consumers can benefit from more selection, certainty of quality, and ease of access at competitive pricing.

This is where the argument of increasing the scope of FDI in the retail space comes into focus. As you can see, expanding FDI limits benefits not only investor sentiment but also reduces manufacturing costs (thereby lowering inflation) through improved supply chain management and elimination of middlemen. Apart from that, the new standards set by large multinational retailers helps in the standardisation of production, technology, packaging, vendor support and quality, all of which can later synergise in the development of domestic versions of Wal-Mart. As mentioned previously, as members of the Indian Collective, we Indians are the experts of indigenisation, and there will be enormous benefits for the Indian retail industry. It can be argued that retail business (both organised and unorganised) contributes close to 10 percent of our GDP. According to a research article published by PTI, it is estimated that the true potential of the Indian retail space is more than $265 billion (some estimates put the figure at $600 billion) and with increased FDI, this target can be achieved by the year 2020 itself! Immense potential isn't it? Not only this, the same article goes on to point out the fact that FDI in retail will roughly create about 10 million (both direct and indirect) jobs and increase government income by $40 billion annually.

While allowing the scope of FDI in retail in the vicinity of 51 percent, the government might want to put in checks and balances in making the indigenous sourcing mandatory for sale in India. According to many media and market studies, prominent multibrand stores such as Wal-Mart and Coirfure source close to 90 percent of their inventory domestically. Thus, several critics' concerns may be alleviated by simple government rules that monitor how much commerce has shifted overseas at the expense of Indian produce. Moreover, it must also be understood that India is a WTO signatory, which means that import and export (international business) concerning India has to be dealt under two categories, NAMA (Non Agricultural Market Access) and Agriculture. Better still, under these contracts enforced by WTO signatories, it is not possible to profitably import goods into a country that are not allowed under the agreement.

India being part of the developing consortium of nations has blocked negotiations several times in order to safeguards its domestic small-scale industry, which may be destroyed by cheap foreign competition (referred to as dumping). With such safeguards already in place and with several others being implemented as part of the process of expanding the scope of FDI, Indian farmers, small scale businessmen and craftsmen can remain assured about the continuity of their livelihood. Brazil is a case in point here, according to *Businessweek* article, *Why Wal-Mart hasn't Conquered Brazil*—large-scale retailing does not guarantee high consumer confidence and profitability. India, are you listening?

Indian Milk Cooperatives Clearly Market Leaders, Why Fear?*

Snapshot: Major Indian Milk Procurers	Notable Brands	Company Type	Daily Milk Procurement (in Litres)
Tamil Nadu Cooperative Milk Producers Federation (TNCMPF)	Aavin	Indian Cooperative	2,683,000[15]
Gujarat Cooperative Milk Marketing Federation (GCMMF)	Amul	Indian Cooperative	13,200,000[16]
Bihar State Cooperative Milk Producers (COMFED)	Sudha	Indian Cooperative	2,000,000[17]
Rajasthan Cooperative Dairy Federation (RCDF)	Saras	Indian Co-operative	2,245,000[18]
Nestle India	Nestle Milk	Multi National	900,000[19]
Haryana Dairy Development Co-operative (HDDC)	Vita	Indian Cooperative	800,000*

*Source: Author's Research; based on 2015 data

The Monetary Mantra

Since the best thoughts are imbibed into the India Collective, it is imperative that a positive feel-good mood is maintained; for this to happen, conducive market-oriented situation is important to prevail in India. This is where the monetary side proponents have their revenge.

If Brazil's monetary policy is analysed closely it reveals that the country has had high interest rates for a long time primarily because it has had the problem of high inflation. In recent history, with almost

12-13 percent interest rate, the Brazilian Central Bank was clearly blocking out private investment for the sake of aiding deficit spending and reducing inflation. Talking through a monetary perspective (Austrian School of Economics), the country's policy makers were with the view that an increased G (Government Expenditure) will bring about more money supply into the economy and will put money in government-enabled projects thereby creating jobs and raise standards of living. At the same time, the high interest rates would deter excessive private investment function and consumption, thereby controlling inflation.

Even though Brazil is one of the few countries in the world that has a relatively stable food price index (the number one contributor of inflation in India), until recently, its Central Bank had continued with its policy of monetary tightening. High interest rates have led to a situation in Brazil where growth is contained in the name of controlling inflation and the economy continues to grow at less than 4 percent per annum for the last four decades. With a diverse economy that includes a healthy mix of high-tech industry, fast expanding and innovative agriculture, new-found oil and gas avenues, the Brazilian economy should have ideally reached the critical point of being termed developed. Sadly, however, the country is still an upper middle-income country with per capita incomes still hovering close to $11,000 (nominal).

A country that records a population growth of almost 2 percent per annum and a 4 percent economic growth may struggle to eliminate inequities as readily as projected, despite the fact that the country has a well-developed and innovative economy to start with. The example of Brazil, a country that is fairly easier to organise given a relatively homogeneous cultural, language and religious affinity clearly shows that growth cannot be compromised in the name of controlling inflation as, often proved, the high interest rate–low growth relationship can be counterproductive. A rising crime rate is a case in point in the Brazil example. This happens mainly because the faulty relationship has only widened the gap between the haves and the have-nots everywhere in the world. If Brazil followed a free-market policy and allowed interest rates to be governed by market forces (along with higher reserve requirements for commercial banks) with periodic fiscal intervention, the state of the nation would have been well different. To add to the argument, if this was to be the case with India in the near future, then four decades of low growth would destroy the natural fabric of our country given its complex demographic and caste-based issues. It is critical to recognise that the Indian Collective is a work in progress and that, among the BRIC countries, only India is a domestic demand-driven economy (our economy depends largely on our own consumption and not on the vagaries of foreign consumers).

Therefore, the above argument states that while Indian central bank (RBI) must allow market forces to govern interest rates, it should leave room for periodic intervention (by virtue of its right to exercise an independent monetary policy). At this critical juncture of the Indian dream, growth cannot be stifled in the name of inflation targeting, primarily because no extra jobs can be created in an environment where interest rates remain persistently higher than necessary. This happens when private sector backed industrial activity is cut off from its two most important pillars of sustenance—one being Consumption function and the other the Investment function.

The argument of the Monetary side proponent rests on the following belief system: 'Persistent High Interest Rates= Possible Stagflation = Purpose Defeated'

Persistent High Interest Rates= *Savings become more appealing to citizens as they get more return on their Fixed Deposits (FD)—Consumption becomes less appealing because more money has to be paid by way of interest rates and higher interest obligations for manufacturers, who are forced to make their products more expensive (making them less appealing to buy, fanning inflation)—Investment in the Stock market is less* *appealing, as investment in stock market is a risky proposition and if the average returns come very close to the prevailing hurdle rates, investors do not foresee a need to take that extra risk (for example, at this time, in India, the cost of equity (assuming that the Equity Risk Premium being 4.5%) is about 7 percent, hurdle rate is about 4 percent and actual nominal Return on Equity is just 3.4 percent, taking extra risk becomes less appealing)—This leads to poor demand for industrial output—No new employment is created by the Industry — No innovation takes place as research funding is cut (due to lack of capital in the market as IPOs fail and external borrowings becomes Expensive/ Elusive)—Risk appetite of new entrepreneurs' declines—Economy stagnates—Higher unemployment and higher inflation—Demand/Supply Disequilibrium* ***—Stagflation-Purpose Defeated.***

We have recently witnessed the negative repercussions of this predicament on our financial system and consumer mentality as a result of years of a high rate regime. It is not nebulous to see that banks have become increasingly wary of consumer loans so much so that in 2012 (a high-rate phase), total disbursements declined by a whopping 20 percent within a matter of 6 months. Bank loans declined from Rs. 8,800 crore disbursement to Rs. 7,000 crore in this period as Non-Performing Assets (NPAs) on Bank Balance Sheets increased to 1.28 percent from 0.97 percent. By 2014, NPAs increased and hovered near the 4 percent mark. Even though the NPA figures are half of what we see today, they sure provide a glimpse of a situation when assets started to go bad. Contrarily though, some economists argue that this is due not only because to a risk-averse banking system, but also to a future risk-averse consumer. Talk about ill effects of prolonged high interest rates.

Looking at the rest of the world, interest rates in the US and the EU are extremely low (hovering at about 1 percent), reflecting not only the abundance of money but also the West's desire to avoid a repeat of the Great Depression of 1931. On comparing today's situation to that of the 1931 economic crises, we find that the situation was somewhat similar. There was a significant time of monetary easing through the 1920s and credit was cheaply available; this situation resulted in significant bad debt in bank balance sheets (as people invested in risky deals because credit was cheap). On hearsay people lost faith in the financial strength of their commercial banks, leading to Bank Runs. This caused a deflationary situation in the US prior to the events that caused the Great Depression, and the Central Bank (Federal Reserve) tried to contain this malady through a sudden increase in interest rates. However, this too was counterproductive since consumers who had borrowed money at lower interest rates suddenly found themselves under significantly more debt and in a bad economic condition, which led to further defaults causing more Bank Runs.

Ultimately, the rich became richer, and poor became poorer (Thomas Pickety's famous inequality function: Rate of return on capital > Economic growth) and the same situation will arise in the present crises if interest rate remain persistently high.*

India cannot simply survive a situation like this; hunger and despair lead to dreadful things and that includes all sorts of social evils. Therefore, feel-good revolutions such as the one that occurred in the telecom sector in the 1990s is all that is required to propagate that all-important and positive 'alpha thought' that binds the nation and a scenario of no growth, but somewhat controlled inflation will jeopardise this healthy processing: for the sake of high growth, lower interest rates are mandatory. As an example, before liberalisation, there was a huge lacuna between the people who owned a fixed-line phone and those who did not and this alienated a sense of empowerment among the general populace and resulted in a feeling of dejection among the have-nots in this country. This feeling of disgruntlement was only alleviated post 1993-94, when telecommunications became more reachable, and this empowered people. Therefore, a no-growth scenario will thus add to dejection and make matters worse for India; something that is least required at this time because growth today is nothing less than the catharsis of the Indian thought. It must be understood that both economics and finance are not understood and governed by numbers but by public sentiment and prevalent mass psychology. However, there is a thin line between a perfect fiscal monetary policy balance and imbalance, which we must first analyse from both perspectives.

I believe that the first wave of Indian self-belief was inculcated by the telecommunications and eventual IT& BPO revolutions after the liberalisation of the Indian economy in the last decade of the twentieth century. The Green revolution and project Flood (Anand co-operative movement under the leadership of Mr. Kurien) that preceded this revolution deserve a respected mention, but none could replicate the chutzpah brought about by the telecom sector. The capability to communicate just about anywhere and anytime was a liberating feeling for most Indians and was perhaps the first nuance proclaiming an end to the License Raj. To express the feeling of pride and joy as experienced by middle-class Indians, I remember entertaining an NRI relative (one who returned to his motherland after a 20-year stint abroad) in our home in 2003. The ensuing actions and reactions resulted in a concoction of exclamations, awe and pride.

Apparently the relative wanted to make a call to his wife in the United States and asked my father to book his call-in advance (as it used to happen in the days prior). To the strange request my father inquired whether the former wanted to book flight tickets in advance in order to save money! Hilarity ensued when the former picked up the phone to dial up the operator—an attempt which was futile to say the least. I still remember the great pride in my father's voice when he politely, but assertively, informed the gentleman that he could call anyone in any part of the world by directly dialling the number he so wishes. "You see, India is now a modern country," my father exclaimed, to which the relative responded with a flabbergasted look and no words. It's the instances like these that have brought about the new-found confidence and the renewal of the Indian ideals (read: India Collective).

This is precisely what growth does to people. Not the big things that bring instant material gain and economic well-being, but the small things that are conversation starters.

So, when certain economists argue that India must control its growth for the sake of inflation management, I can't help but wonder whether the arguing gentlemen ever spent time at a tea stall with a couple of strangers? You see, India as a nation is very different from the other emerging economies it is so clubbed with these days. Most Indian people have emerged from the clutches of poverty through hard work and grit and do not wish to glorify their struggles through the hard times. The depressing times may be expressed with a pinch of salt and patented Indian humour, but it's still considered a more personal issue to be shared with 'just met' strangers. The post-liberalised India is very different to the India of the past. With increased interregional movement of labour/workers, cigarette acquaintances are no longer those with whom people grow up with but strangers who they meet while working and chat up during the frequent cigarette/*bidi* breaks. If you take out growth from the new-found feel good equation, you effectively eliminate any positive dialogues, and let me emphasise that my argument is not limited to the educated elite.

*By the way, there is a very little chance that there will be Bank Runs in India as most Indian Commercial Banks are nationalised (guaranteed and owned by the government). Monetary tightening led bad-debt problem will create lower margins and more write off for the banks but there may never really be a Bank-Run type of a situation here.

BSE 100 Movement, 1991-2020: Based on Market Mood

Year	Closes	India's Mood Induced Market Movement
1991	518.1	Liberalization of the Indian Economy/Several trade policies Implemented/Import Duty Cuts
1992	687.07	Private Airlines were allowed, heralding a new Indian Aviation policy
1993	935.91	FIls are allowed to trade in the Indian Market/National Telecom Policy (NTP) announced to attract FDI into the Indian Telecom Sector/Prithvi Test Fire Successful

1994	1080.98	
1995	829.84	
1996	790.78	First visit of a Chinese state Head to India as President Jiang Zemin visits New Delhi
1997	920.23	
1998	788.24	Nuclear Tests (Pokhran 1998) National Highway Development Project (NHDP) establish/Announcement of the Golden Quadrilateral (GQ) National Highway Network
1999	1522.2	Sanctions on India duw to Nuclear Tests
2000	1178.68	Indian Growth Rate declines from 7% to 5.8%/Telecom Workers Protest following nationalization of the Department of Telecommunications
2001	903.19	India enters the elite club with the capability of Geosynchronous Satellite Launch/of the Sarva Siksha Abhiyan
2002	965.51	Delhi Metro Unleashed (Major push to infrastructure and announcement for other major cities also)
2003	1783.42	Prime Minister Vajpayee visits China. All time high for Indo-China Relations
2004	2076.6	India and Russia sign the Vikramaditya Deal. India set to acquire its new Aircraft Carrier
2005	2872.9	India Wins ODI Series in Pakistan (Market mood upbeat)
2006	4049.88	International Band width prices reduced by 70% by TRA/ International Direct Dialing to several regions reduced by 33%
2007	6469.48	Nandigram Violence-Corporate trust in Government Policy shaken/ Samjhauta Express Bombings
2008	2893.06	The US House of Representative clears the US-India Civil Nuclear Deal/ Chandrayan-1 Lunar Mission Launched
2009	4675.04	India's first indigenously developed Nuclear Submarine (INS Arihant) Launched
2010	6191.51	
2011	5941.7	India wins ICC World Cup 2011 (Market mood upbeat)
2012	5148.02	
2014	7473.5	NDA comes to power; market anticipates business friendly policies.
2015	8097.6	
2016	8796.1	Demonetization exercise brought about tremendous investable liquidity
2020	9951.3	Advent of the Covid-19 crises; accommodative monetary policy, cheap money

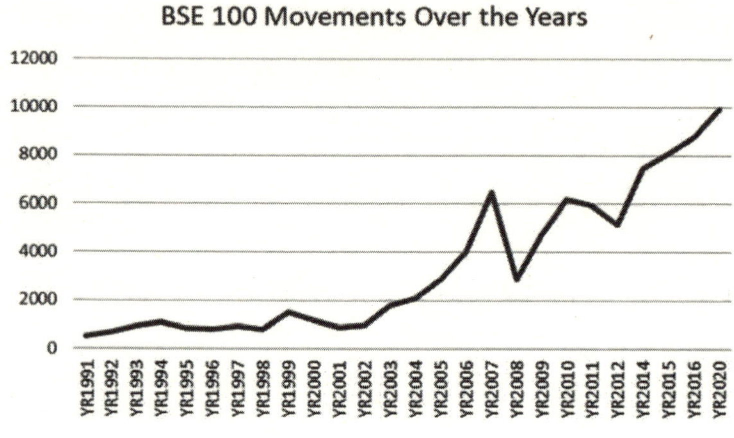

Source: Author's Research

India's Keynesian Conflict

In March 2013, with its decision to reduce the REPO rate by 25 basis points, to everyone's surprise, the Reserve Bank of India (RBI) had apparently become docile and pro-markets for a change. Experts believed that the astonishing but true alteration in Dr. Subbarao's attitude from being a ruthless crusader against inflation to a messiah of market forces had a direct connection to India's flop show in the much-coveted GDP growth competitions. These figures were not only the performance measurement of the government, but also yardsticks of where we stood as a nation in terms of socio-economic well-being. Given the economy's one of the worst performances in a decade, there seemed to be no respite for India as a looming sub 5 percent growth rate threatened to jeopardise the country's plans to have an equitable and long-lasting growth.

Dr. Raghuram Rajan, the Governor at the time, was similarly dissatisfied, as his predecessor, when his regime persisted with the 'crusader' bit. If we look at the sentiment of the market, it was clear that India's once bullish private sector wasn't happy anymore; interestingly, the stock market crash did not tell the full story. Because of high interest rates of the time and flagging demand doing the rounds, private fixed investment had considerably declined as the private sector did not expect demand to pick up in the short to medium term. Theoretically, in such tricky situations, a lack of augmentation to the manufacturing capacity will not lead to economies of scale, and prices will in effect increase further. The RBI had put up a brave face during the time but its later hinting at a possible quantitative easing had raised questions regarding the country's fiscal–monetary harmony. Suddenly, India's central bank was thinking differently and no longer believed in the Government's ability to make a difference. It seemed that even though poor economic performance was nothing new for India, the Government had always found refuge in the ideas of John Maynard Keynes, who proposes Government Expenditure to steer Aggregate Demand (AD) and keeping the economy afloat. This appears to be not working anymore and there is a major conflict between the intent and the result.

In essence, AD (also used to calculate the GDP) is often termed as the 'effective demand' as per the Keynesians; in other words, AD is what is eventually demanded rather than what was initially planned. Therefore fundamentally, AD's components are important parameters in measuring the real health of an economy. In an event of an economic slowdown or a recession, AD invariably slides towards the left, signifying the fact that real demand for the goods and services produced by the country has declined.

According to John Maynard Keynes, one of the greatest economists of all time, the government must have a prerogative in lifting demand and getting an economy back on track through what he called 'Fiscal Intervention'. In this situation, when the government sees the economy flagging, it tries to increase Government Expenditure (G) at the cost of Private Consumption (C). As proscribed, the government must generally use this tool in order to perform two functions—one, to take the economic mantle on its own shoulders because it believes that the private sector is not capable enough to bear the burden alone; and two, to restrict private consumption, because higher consumption in a recessionary situation results in inflation as supply is anyway restricted due to reduced Investment (I).

Ideally, the central bank, sensing the government's intentions, increases the interest rates, thus bringing about equilibrium in the country's fiscal and monetary policies. The Investment, Savings, Liquidity Model (IS-LM), which was influenced by Keynes, suggested that on an x, y axis for every rightward fiscal movement, there will be an accompanying leftward monetary movement or vice versa. On these lines, during Fiscal Intervention, the government tries to increase output through its own effort bringing about increased economic activity, employment opportunities, higher incomes and output-driven lower prices but this is accompanied by an increase in interest rates. Due to the fact that the government needs additional funding to operate and its own resources are insufficient to carry out this perform this massive activity, the former must use public savings (which in India is over $1 trillion). A high interest rate allows the government to get access to higher funding as higher interest rates increase the propensity to save and consume less among the general population. This massive exercise is a short- to medium-term stabilising mechanism, and its central idea is to get things back on track.

INDIA'S KEYNESIAN CONFLICT

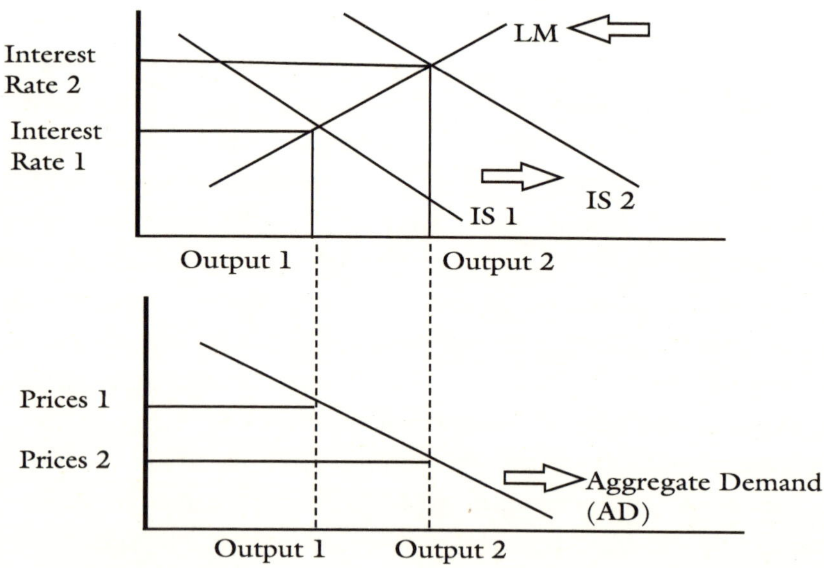

Compiled by: Author

It is important to understand that the AD is output driven and in an event of fiscal intervention, prices must go down thereby increasing demand. This happens because an increased production on the back of an increased G and the accompanying Multiplier Effect will bring about economies of scale. As per the Keynesian model, when the government takes the onus of reviving the economy on itself, it results in a win-win situation for the economy as higher economic activity creates higher employment opportunities. As a consequence, incomes not only rise but higher production leads to lower prices and higher demand for goods and services in the long run, bringing about an economic recovery of sorts.

However, there is a catch in this simple 'pedantic' approach as the economy where it is implemented must be exporting more than it is importing. Aggregate Demand is essentially a function of Investment (I), Consumption (C), Government Expenditure (G) and the difference between Exports and Imports. For countries like China and Germany, who have surplus economies, this type of fiscal intervention is often successful and actually stimulates demand; but in countries such as India, where deficits are the norm, the envisaged effects may not bring desired results. Here the effects of a deficit have a negative outcome on the aggregate demand and government expenditure becomes the only variable that actually drives demand.

Until recently, India had faced the problem of extreme low growth complemented by high interest rates because the Keynesian model is apparently not working here. We may have a situation in India in which the revival of the economy is no longer carried by fiscal interventions and which may have even negative influences. Plan Expenditure 2013-14, for example, even though increased, had to get access to extra funds through cuts in other important allocated budgets such as defence. It is about time that we realise that our past beliefs stemming from our 'Mixed Economy' mentality no longer function as effectively as they once used to. In all probability, market forces should definitely be given a chance to prove their mantle, just as John Maynard Keynes must give way to Adam Smith.

Premise of the Monetary Mantra and India's Keynesian Conflict

Being an acolyte of the Austrian School of Economics and greats such as Ludwig Von Mises and Carl Menger, and later Eugen Von Boehm-Bawerk, I am also with the view that interest rates are not an 'artificial construct' and so cannot justifiably influence public sentiment when it comes to consumption of capital. Therefore, I believe that 'artificially modulating' interest rates cannot 'artificially subdue' demand for capital but merely postpone it. After a policy review meeting in August 2014, defending his hawkish stance, Dr. Raghuram Rajan, the 23rd Governor of the Reserve Bank of India (RBI), was reported in an interview with the Times of India as saying, "We are not against growth, but we feel that growth will be most benefited if we disinflate the economy and we don't have to fight this fight again. Let us fight the anti-inflation fight once and let us win." Going by that logic it seems that the governor, whose lecture on Macro Economics greatly influenced me while I was a student at *Frankfurt*, feels that high interest rates are necessary to fight inflation in a country that is held for ransom by supply side constraints. With that reasoning, I can't help but wonder whether high interest rates are the 'artificial solutions' to a 'structural problem'? Maybe I am wrong in gauging the structural realities of the economy, but the RBI cannot forever protect the government's fiscal incompetence while tormenting private investors. Using interest rates for maintaining competitive yield differentials is a different story though.

Eugen Von Boehm-Bawerk in his acclaimed 1884 work, *History and Critique of Interest Theories* articulates that interest rates are an inherent part of the market representing "the universal fact of 'time preference' (discount rate)."[1]

Perhaps, based on my own interpretation of this theory, I believe when central banks artificially play with interest rates to merely fight inflation, they overlook the fact that the hoarders/owners of capital not only become wealthier (also pointed out by Thomas Pikitty in his book *Capital in the Twenty First Century*), but perceptually also become risk averse! If interest rates indeed are a construct of the market then high interest rates fixed by central banks help create a façade that capital owners are no longer interested in lending out capital to the market as they exhibit 'high' time preferences and therefore demand higher discount rates. However, in reality there is no such phenomenon occurring in a free market as central banks rarely take into account the concerns of the capital owners while fixing interest rates. Therefore, while creating this façade, high interest rates fundamentally conflict the interests of capital owners, who are not able to derive a greater value from their capital in a booming economy where higher capital is employed. Under all circumstances, the high interest rates play havoc with business plans to increase investment—especially CAPEX (Capital Expenditure)—which is a signal of economic expansion and hence more jobs.

By maintaining historically high interest rates, RBI, like other hawkish central banks, until recently believed that it is defending the economy from inflationary pressures ignoring the real concerns of a market that is reeling under supply side deficiencies. Merely subduing demand for capital may temporarily alleviate the problem of excess consumption, but as this pent-up demand will resurface with a with a vengeance in the medium to long term, this is no viable solution. If economic expansion is allowed to take care of demand supply disequilibrium as a natural course of action, then it will also take care of the supply side induced inflationary pressures. All said and done, high rates are certainly no nukes to end a world war. These are, at best, meek signals.

Counter to a Free-Market Interest Rate Policy

While rationalising high interest rates and how they play havoc with a developing country's ability to build sustainable ecosystems, naturally there were certain perspectives that forced me to think otherwise as well. Taking the example of South East Asian countries such as Thailand, Malaysia and, recently, Philippines, it is quite clear that low interest rates, which perpetually follow market sentiment, can also be counterproductive. In the above mentioned countries, interest rates trailing at sub 3 percent levels have made credit cheap and therefore often unproductive. With rising Non Performing Assets (NPAs) in bank balance sheets, the debt to GDP burden in the mentioned countries is rising so much so that certain sections of economists are auguring a repeat of the dreaded 1996-97 Financial Crises.[2] However, if we try to equate the fallacies related to low interest rates in India's case, we must understand that at 10 percent range, NPAs in our banking system are much higher than even these countries. Therefore, it might be difficult to correlate low interest rate with borrower delinquency as we face the problem with perceptually 'prohibitive' hurdle rates. Arguing from both perspectives, even though a loose monetary policy may lead to a higher defaulter rate in the financial system, it certainly may not be a major concern for India as here the problem is capacity constraint. High defaults are due to a higher burden of high interest rates and not delinquent behaviour (this might be equated to a repeat situation of the 1931 Great Depression where high interest rates after high liquidity destroyed the market at its core).

Notes

1. http://mises.org/etexts/austrian.asp (Author and Publication: Mises Institute/ Date: 2007-01-08)
2. http://www.bloombergview.com/articles/2014-08-0 4/asia-s-next-crisis-is-a-flood-of-debt (Author: William Pesek/ Publication: Bloomberg / Date: 2018-8-4)

The Demographic Farce

In the early 2000s, there were alarming unemployment rates recorded in some of Europe's most advanced economies. With an average of over 9 percent, sociologists and economists realised that socioeconomic development alone could not cure all societal problems. While development may result in fundamental changes to the way a society functions, it cannot be an end in itself. It was later revealed that increased mechanisation was one of the primary reasons behind the prevalent unemployment rates because development spawns mechanisation, which leads to efficiency and naturally high levels of automation results. Therefore, work that was traditionally done by humans was now done by machines making people effectively redundant.

This was the time when former German Chancellor Gerhard Schroeder brought about sweeping yet painful labour reforms that offered the suffocated industry a window of hope.[20] Even in the current economic crisis, especially in the resultant Euro crisis, the employment rates have been the first casualty with some countries recording over 30 percent unemployment, with youngsters finding it almost impossible to find meaningful work. Interestingly even though Europe has been reeling under negative birth rates with more deaths than live births, the continent's most advanced countries are finding themselves in this quagmire. Consider India, where replacement rates have always exceeded and will continue to do so in the short to medium term, with some analysts putting the date of stabilisation (replacement rates at less than 2) somewhere in the year 2080, a dangerous socioeconomic disturbance seems inevitable.

As an example, the National Sample Survey (NSS) 66th Round data from the Indian Ministry of Statistics and Programme Implementation indicates that India has 476 people under the age of 30 for every 1000 inhabitants. Even if half of these young people are employable and actively seeking work, India needs develop at least 250'sustainable' jobs along the economic value chain for every

500 under-30s. Also, as per the survey's 'usual principal approach' the average labour participation in India is 558 (accounting for both males and females in urban–rural settings) out of a total every 1000 people. This means that if there are 1200 million people living in India, the country has 670 million people eager to work at all 'sample' times, a figure that is substantially more than the estimated 500 million existing labour force. It is therefore clear that the Indian economy lacks the sufficient scale to create enough jobs, and even if it did, it would certainly not guarantee creation of sufficient jobs (because the European example is still fresh in our minds). In all probability, we don't need so many 'hands' to experience a demographic dividend; the fixation around a high population being a boon for our economy is nothing more than a political propaganda. Productivity will no longer be related to population in the next decade as a result of rising mechanisation. In the near future, the younger demographic dividend is a myth as quality of life improves, people will live longer and have more productive years to contribute.

As our economy evolves further, our industry will develop and adapt newer global standards and automation will hold the key towards efficiency. As Foreign Direct Investment (FDI), Foreign Institutional Investment increases and Indian companies additionally get more access to capital through their global operations, Indian economy will slowly but steadily transform itself into a capital-intensive economy from its erstwhile labour-intensive avatar. In such circumstances, the country will find its labour force redundant, especially because over 95 percent of workers are unorganised, mostly devoid of any technical skill set striving in a job market where specialisation holds the key. As an instance, Amitabh Kant, the CEO& MD of Delhi–Mumbai Industrial Corridor (DMIC), stated in a *Times of India* editorial that the country will add 138 million workers to the working-age population by the year 2020-21. He also mentioned that the National Manufacturing Policy (NMP) of India envisions an increase of industrial sector's contribution to 25 percent (from current 16 percent) in the next ten years for which a sustained industrial growth of 16 percent is required; short change required by India to achieve Chinese levels of industrialisation, isn't it? Going by that logic, industrialisation is the key towards creating sustainable jobs for the Indian work force because that alone can provide on-the-job training to 'less educated-unskilled' labour category, that is predominant in India. One reason cited for India being overwhelmingly dependent economically on the service sector is the fact that a service-driven economy does not only include high-end information technology services but all kinds of services that can be rendered by 'any willing person' without any prerequisite skills; some examples of dominant service sector jobs include guards, *presswallas*, casual workers or drivers.

Clearly, with the exception of a few high-end businesses, the service sector does not rely on skill development for survival, since there is enough of casual work available, which is why it thrives in its current form here. Probably in India, the term 'disguised unemployment' was used to characterise such individuals. It must be realised that the Indian economy is not mature enough to rely solely on the service sector for job creation, as India's service sector lacks the innovation and specialisation to create meaningful value and disburses prosperity that can actually percolate.

Some may argue that because the economic distribution of the developed world is overwhelmingly dependent on the service sector, there is little reason to complain about India. The reason being simple, no country in the world leapfrogged the industrial renaissance towards economic prosperity; the Western countries have gradually graduated to services because manufacturing 'on their behalf ' is now done by low-cost destinations (which makes business sense), while they concentrate on the operational side of the business only as sufficient specialisations in the economy develop. As an example, even though China manufacturers the Apple iPhone, it only manages to earn less than 5 percent of the total unit sale price;

the rest mainly goes to the patent holder country, you guessed it right, USA. India under all circumstances has to go down the same road and there is no other choice.

Industrialisation (secondary) sector thus is the only way forward as industry needs skill development for its sustainability as technology changes often and worker skills must be updated with changing times. However, scale here is the key. As mentioned earlier, services with present socioeconomic conditions will not solve India's development issues, but a renewed focus on industrialisation with a special concentration on volume (scale) will give a complete picture.

Therefore, if Narendra Modi, former Chief Minister of Gujarat and the 15th Indian Prime Minister, in his speech at Delhi's Shri Ram College of Commerce and Pune's Fergusson College, points out the importance of scale in Indian industry, he is absolutely right and understands India's underlying development equation. Fortunately, the Planning Commission on its part has identified the problem and the 12th Five Year Plan has had a renewed focus on Skill Development, and has allocated Rs. 2200 crore for the same in the budget of the financial year 2013. However, for these initiatives to become a reality and successfully solve the identified problems, we must understand how such an exercise can be undertaken, and population control holds the utmost urgency.

Whether we keep these facts on the back burner for now, while these figures stare us in the face? If not dealt with in the near future, this massive deluge of eligible workers will break the very backbone of the India Collective's social fabric, and the government and corporate machinery will fail to provide meaningful employment under all circumstances. These structural problems of India must be rectified in order to unleash the India Collective's true potential, or it may be too late to start.

"New technologies, methods of production and means of distribution make old ones obsolete, forcing companies to quickly adapt to new environment or fail."

—Joseph Schumpeter, Austrian Economist

The Fixation with Standardised Education

The OECD's *Program for International Student Assessment* (PISA) 2009 found that Indian 15-year olds were the worst performing subjects among the children of 74 tested nations. Indian 15-year olds were not only found to be the worst in their knowledge of the sciences but were also second last in traditionally strong subjects such as mathematics! Result? According to *Higher Education in India: 12th Five Year Plan and Beyond Report* (a joint venture between the erstwhile *Planning Commission, FICCI, E&Y*), India records one of the lowest *'Gross Enrolment Ratios'* (GER) in the world. As compared to the GER global average of 27 percent, India records a dismal 16 percent. Moreover, the report signifies the fact that most of the institutions of higher learning fare badly in NAAC Accreditations; with almost 90 percent of the accredited institutions being average or below average. This could be because of education being a low priority in our national outlay/planned expenditure. Most assume that while education should have a renewed refocus with increased allocations by the Government, only 4.1 percent (as per NationMaster) of the GDP is earmarked towards it. Also, to make matters worse, according to UNDP, India has one of the world's lowest expenditures per student in higher education; a very standardised blame game that very conveniently steers clear from the crux of the issue because everybody seems to forget the primary and secondary education systems.

As per several experts I have been talking to regarding education systems in India and some of my own terrible experiences while at school, there seems to be a fixation towards standardisation, which in this case is inversed to our collective. It seems that the effective Indian *Gurukula* system of yore got horribly influenced by the early British Public School system of the nineteenth century, where pedantic standardised education was the norm. Just like everything else, our Collective absorbed and tried to standardise this relatively new system of education but apparently the process of **integration** didn't go as expected. Before the British arrived, the Indian education system revolved around the absolute authority of a teacher, who was in turn a master of his subject through practice. The post-Renaissance British school system, however, revolved around textbooks, which were written by somebody else (not the teacher himself/herself) and presented a standardised literature to be memorised without much creativity involved. Even though the British education evolved further into a 'facilitator' style system, where the teachers became mere facilitators to student learning processes, India was stuck in the quagmire of having a confused, strict and standardised structure. In the modern Indian education system, while the teacher remained the central provider of knowledge, the body of knowledge was somewhere else, in standardised textbooks. As a result of this system, the Indian education system was a provider of education that lacked the required level of imagination and originality for success, which resulted in the country becoming a poor incubator of innovation. After Independence, when the Plan Policy framework was formulated, higher education became the Government's new focus while the K12 (primary school to Class XII) was somewhat ignored. As a result of this apathy, the school education system continued to evolve into its present form unhindered. I think most of our creative thinkers, achievers, writers and innovators became what they eventually became once they graduated our higher education institutions and safely ensconced themselves away from our dreaded schools. This is precisely the reason why we never had a Bill Gates or a Steve Jobs, two men who dropped out of college but became master innovators. Our brain drain spawns creative maelstroms in Western countries when brilliant NRIs make huge money by merely expressing their years of suppressed creativity; why can't that happen here in India?

In order to be more flexible and spawn future innovation, India has to change its structured educational curriculum to a choice-based system in which students can study whatever they desire. The problem with Indian primary and secondary education system is that it is extremely pedantic and inflexible. Because they cannot choose between subjects, students from a young age try to fit into the structured curriculum at school, depriving themselves of what actually interests and stimulates them. Due to this fixated nature of our education, we are actually depriving our nation of promising sportsmen, writers, artists and diplomats who get lost in standardisation. A 1.35 billion strong nation managing a dismal 6 Olympic medals is a case in point here (if lack of infrastructure is your counter-answer then the comparative medal tally of certain low- income African countries can put things in perspective!). A particular young CEO who came to India because he wanted to contribute to the Indian growth story had to return to America because his son complained that his school does not let him choose between subjects. The promising Indian professional could not help his son, who was adamant that he did not want to study Chemistry in Class VIII. It is difficult to comprehend the fact that in standardised schools, a student cannot study a combination of Physics, Medieval European History, Theatre, Mathematics, Geography and Philosophy in Class XII? For reasons unknown.

The Gold Standard: 'Language'

In November 1954, Pakistani leaders envisaged an ingenious plan to unite the country's disparate territories on India's Eastern and Western frontiers. The Western part, current-day Pakistan, was a concoction of the Punjabi-dominated Punjab Province, the Sindhi-dominated Sindh, the Baloch territory of Baluchistan and the unruly Pathan (Pashtun)-dominated North Western Frontier Provinces (NWFP). On the other hand, the Eastern part, present- day Bangladesh, was a predominantly ethnic Bengali territory. Even though all territories were overwhelmingly Muslim, people of these different regions were diverse and were fiercely protective of their cultures and languages.

Confronted with the challenges of administering such a wide expanse of territory in a country founded on religion, the Pakistani leadership at the time was adamant that religion was perhaps the only uniting factor of the new country. With this belief system, the then Chief of Army Staff, General Ayub Khan and Minister of Interior, Iskandar Mirza devised a plan to bring about 'Collectivity' in East and West Pakistan. The plan, termed *'The One Unit Program'* was to be the blueprint of modern Pakistan and was envisaged to bring about unity among all citizens irrespective of their ethnicity. As per the plan, Western Pakistan, with all its diversity would be called, West Pakistan while on the other hand East Bengal was to be called as East Pakistan. Both regions were to be governed independently by two capital cities, Lahore (West Pakistan) and Dacca (East Pakistan), which were to have elected senates reporting directly to the central legislature positioned at a new national capital territory, Islamabad. The plan appeared brilliant on paper and seemed to work initially as management became easier and chain of command became more effective for maximum policy implementation. Pakistani leaders, Iskandar Mirza and Ayub Khan became examples of the new system as their very own unique power-sharing equation was seemingly working even though the former was an ethnic Bengali while the latter was a Pashtun.

However, this standardisation exercise did not work as planned because standardisation also brought about the standardisation of language and culture. If ensure the Ayub–Mirza plan's genuine success, people must speak a standard language and practice a common cultural system. I think the Pakistani leaders believed that they could do for Pakistan what Mustafa Kemal Ataturk did for Turkey. In this aping however, the Pakistanis forgot one simple fact: the Turks were not only predominantly Muslim but were also culturally homogenous (after the break-up of the Ottoman Empire and division through the Franco–British led 1945 Palestinian Mandate). Pakistan, on the other hand, was not culturally or racially homogeneous in any sense. The One Unit programme gradually imposed the Punjabified Urdu language and culture on the rest of the country and problems started erupting from there onwards. The Bengalis and Balochs were the first to get offended from this blatant indigenous cultural massacre in the name of unity and soon independent factions took up protests and public dismay was hugely apparent on the streets. Power-sharing agreements between the West and East political forces failed miserably and the Easterners found themselves to be the victims in their own country. The state retaliated and armed oppressions at the hands of the military brought about events such as the resurrection of the independent rebel army, *Mukti Bahini* in East Pakistan and eventually its fight for freedom. The One Unit programme was finally abandoned in the year 1970, on fears of losing East Pakistan; however, it was too late to react as the damages were irreversible.

We in India inherited the same unmanageable diversity (sometimes even more) as did Pakistan, but fortunately we never considered our diversity as a curse. Instead, the modern secular Indian constitution incorporated respect for all religions and ethnicities so much so that the Constitution's 8th Schedule identifies and recognises 22 different languages in order to represent all Indians. Dr. Bhim Rao Ambedkar, the father and architect of Indian Constitution predominantly focused on one overbearing fact—peaceful coexistence and respect for all cultures among citizens. True to the values ascribed by our forefathers, since its modern inception, India never stood for any particular religion, language or culture and thankfully our modern founders understood that fact well. Thus, India's Collective is founded on diversity, and our continued existence as a 'one country' state is living proof.

We probably survived because we never enforced a thing like the One Unit Programme in our diverse country, where a language changes every 50 miles but that may not be a good thing forever. One thing I admire about the Pakistanis is the fact that they identified the chief problem of managing a diverse country, the language. While the implementation of their strategy went horribly wrong, they understood their management lessons correctly: for an effective future-proof strategy, an effective chain of command is critical, and diversity must be managed through a standardised means of communication. Here, the examples of the United States and Switzerland come afore. You see, even the United States is a diverse country like ours and is rightly described as an 'immigrant's country' yet the standard means of communication is English. The best part about the American system is that there is no real enforcement but for the sake of the entire community, there has to be a language which is somewhat universally understood or aspired. Since, people who immigrate to America do not carry their baggage consisting of pre-conceived notions, and do realise and accept what America truly represents, a land of diversity and therefore opportunity. There are several communities that have steadfastly maintained their unique identities through their unique cultures and languages, yet when it comes to intercommunity interaction, English is the only way. In Switzerland, another collectivity-in-diversity model, English is used by the advertisers to standardise communication because the country's Italian, French and German-speaking populations are too proud to speak each other's languages. Apparently, according to the Swiss marketers, the only language capable of effectively engaging with a broad range of audiences is one that nobody speaks (natively)!

In India, for the sake of future planning and for the sake of our collective, we require a means of communication that is standardised for the sake of everyone without offending anyone. The idea is to not take away the peculiar cultural diversity of our nation but to bring about a system where every Indian is on an equal footing through ease of communications. Chandra Bhan Prasad and Milind Kamble of the Dalit Indian Chamber of Commerce and Industry (DICCI) tirelessly advocated for English as India's national language to be spoken by all Indians, including Dalits. If we look closely, there is a lot of merit in what these gentlemen envisage for India. English is probably the only language that has no peculiar affinity to any particular community yet it is widely spoken (and aspired to be spoken). In fact, today India has the largest English-speaking collective population in the world and the country's economic rise (again) is because of this language.

You see, in the case of Pakistan, the East Pakistanis felt humiliated and felt inferior when the language of their brethren in the west was enforced upon them. Had there been a language that had nothing to do with any concerned stakeholder in Pakistan, matters would have been easier to handle. In this case, all stakeholders would have to agree unanimously, and there would be no grudging cultural invasion. We must consider the sweeping change brought about by Mustafa Kemal Ataturk instead as his standardised

'Turkish' language was spoken widely in Turkey and nobody was humiliated by its Westernisation as the language represented the collective Turkish pride. Let English be the language of the modern Indian Collective then.

The Peculiar 'Dustbin'

"Where are you going with all that trash in one bag," asked my land lady. "To throw it away in the dustbin," I replied with a visible sense of responsibility towards my new surroundings. "Well, you have all types of trash in one bag. How on earth will you segregate?" she exclaimed. "Segregate?" I asked with a puzzled look on my face. "Don't you know? Different types of trash go in separate dustbins. Glass goes in Glass Bin, which is at the corner of this street; Bio Degradable Trash will go in Dustbin 1 and non-Bio Degradable Trash will go in Dustbin 2. Also, please take care that you use the bins that belong to our house, don't put the trash in the neighbour's bins or they will get upset!"

Perplexed, I couldn't help but think about the ridiculous fuss over a 'freaked' dustbin of all the things. Even though I came from a complex environment prevalent in India, I never quite understood the momentary lapse of rationality of the so-called developed world. Why on earth would someone create so much complexity around a simple exercise of getting rid of trash? Not able to understand the logic then, I spent the whole day thinking about the concept of 'dustbin' and why they are so important? In my home country, India, nobody cared about dustbins, trash can be thrown anywhere and there are certainly other more important things to deal with, right? Wrong! While going to university early the next day, I saw a trash pickup truck, with two guys diligently picking up the dustbin(s) outside every house and patiently dumping them into the trucks aft. They didn't care to check the contents of each dustbin because they seemed to trust the households to make their jobs easier. Lesson? Simply said, houses separate trash not simply to comply with the law, but also out of genuine concern for the individuals who clean up the area each morning. Do we Indians think on those lines? We all have the answers.

I believe that our lack of civility is also due to the fact that cleanliness was never instilled in us with the same zeal as, say, mathematics and sciences were; there are certain 'chapters' in our civics books at junior school, but apparently it wasn't really that important while preparing our young minds to have a holistic life experience. As a concept, quality of life has always been about achieving more success in life (competing better) and having a clean 'house' or surroundings was never an issue. More than the education, even our governments never took the issue of civil hygiene seriously.

Figuratively speaking though, no one party can be blamed here for the mess as using dustbins (as public convenience and responsibility towards others) is a farfetched scenario for a country where personal hygiene figures somewhere in the last-demand hierarchy for a majority. Undoubtedly, India is witnessing a colossal change and spurt in public infrastructure, yet strangely more Indian people engage in open defecation than those in Africa, either due to a lack of public sanitation services or due to their own lack of concern. Inherently, our country lacks appropriate toilets, resulting in a lack of sanitation, and increasingly, civil groups are recognising the issue. The 'Toilets are Beautiful' campaign,* launched in New Delhi recently, is one such instance where open defecation and sanitation sensitisation is envisioned to solve a crisis-like situation. For long, sanitation facilitation has been a bone of contention between the Central and the state governments, and consensus-building exercises have been bogged due to expense-sharing disagreements. The casualty seems to be an inexpensive yet 'omnipresent' object found everywhere else in the world: 'The Dustbin', which nobody seems to think about! Even though the dustbins will not solve the open defecation problem in this country they will at least give a hang of the 'expectations' of a civil society; have a 'Demonstration Effect' so to say.

Looking around, Indian cities aspiring to become global centres of commerce desperately lack these inexpensive objects of desire. In relation to the investment on public amenities, there seems to be an apathy towards an amenity that will keep the environment cleaner at a low cost. There is never one close by when you really need it the most. Some of us, who know our responsibilities, keep our trash in our pockets until we really find a place to throw it away; often taking the trash elsewhere due to a lack of opportunity—A view shared by eminent Journalist Vinod Mehta in his *Hindustan Times* editorial on missing dustbin. The inculcation of a civic responsibility is possible once there are examples to be followed and by providing 'omnipresent' dustbins; precisely that is what is not done. According to an expert on Urban Planning, the primary reason behind this seemingly lack of interest towards our surroundings comes from a lack of 'peer pressure.' Most of Indian cities are relatively new urban centres, which are the sum of several villages and towns incorporated during the former's expansion. As these expansions were unplanned and continued to attract additional migrants from outside, the central values associated with sustainable urban living were never inculcated, with the simple unit logic prevalent among most urban dwellers being "this is not my place hence I don't care." Now, most of the world's cities probably have the same origins as those in India, but apparently these countries realised it early that urban living is collective living and responsibility lies on all stakeholders involved. Given that this book is about identifying the collectivity within us Indians, it will not be out of sync to say that the modern India Collective 'lacks' the value system associated with responsible urban living, owing to the fact that India was never an urban society and its evolution somehow overlooked the collective civil 'hygiene' clause.

I believe that moral principles will be incorporated if we first understand urban living, which can be accomplished through the provision of basic amenities such as Dustbins/Trash Bins. The 'Peer Pressure' was somehow never inducted into the India Collective because, as stated earlier, urbanisation as a concept is brand new for India. Let's begin the learning process with and through the use of dustbins.

* Launched by Quicksand and WashUnited on World Toilet Day (November 19, 2012)

"Freedom is Not Free"
A Korea War Memorial near Natick
(Massachusetts, US) MBTA Station

Military and International Relations

"A country must function as a well-oiled war machine at all times"

—Anonymous

India's Meiji Restoration

Technology Transfers and Co-Production for Indian Defence needs

When the 1st Air Fleet of the Japanese Imperial Navy left the Hitokappu Base situated in the Japanese archipelago's northernmost island of Hokkaido, there was a lot of thought behind the movement. Contrary to popular opinion, Admiral Isoroku Yamamoto, the Japanese naval strategist, was not gambling when he sought the Emperor's authorisation and masterminded the largest naval movement in history. After all, the 1st Air Fleet consisted of the *Kido Butai*, the world's largest Carrier Battle Group, comprised of 6 aircraft carriers (with accompanying fleets of destroyers, frigates and tankers), over 400 fighter aircrafts (including *Kamikaze* divisions) and 24 submarines. What transpired during the next 15 days altered the course of World War II, as America was coerced into the War. The attack and destruction of the American Base at Pearl Harbor, which killed over 2100 American soldiers and injured several hundred others, had a direct precedent in Japanese insecurity stemming from dependence. Even though the primary reason of the pre-empt strike was Japanese ambitions to control resource-rich South East Asia, there was a great fear lingering in the Japanese psyche at the time. Japan was highly dependent on American machine tools, aircraft assembly, strategic technology and oil, and when American President Franklin D. Roosevelt's Administration voted in favour of an embargo restricting supplies, the Japanese were inconsolably irked.

Yamamoto and his war strategists knew that Japan's dependence on America could cost it dearly in the medium term and the outcome of the War had everything to do with unrestricted supplies of required accoutrements from America. The Japanese believed that a concentrated military effort on a large scale would demoralise the Americans and swiftly bring them to the negotiating table, allowing them to satisfy Japanese demands to restart replenishment lines immediately. Little did the Japanese know, Pearl Harbor's unprovoked massacre acted as a wakeup call for the mighty American war machinery and the rest is history as we know it. Therefore, the reason for the Japanese fear was simple; the Americans were self-sufficient while the Japanese were not. From the time of the Meiji Restoration, which started some 50 years prior to the War, the Japanese had benefited greatly from the newly devised Transfer of Technology (ToT) and Co-production schemes from Europe and America and now had no qualms in getting what they wanted through force or otherwise. America, on the other hand, had a more powerful and developed military complex at the time and the biggest advantage (and Japan's biggest fear) was America's complete 'self-reliance' as a war machine, the deciding factor that contributed greatly to the War's final outcome.

If not sooner, India finds itself at the juncture where Japan found itself during the Meiji Restoration. In a bid towards self-reliance, India can increasingly find itself in Japanese boots during situations where it is held at ransom by those it depends upon. During the Kargil conflict, the economic embargo on India resulted in restricted supply of ammunitions from several partner countries causing several artillery equipment lying useless. Of course, India would not summon its undersized vintage INS Virat or relatively unproven INS Vikramaditya-led Carrier Battle Groups (CBG) in trying to get answers to its vindictive questions. The geopolitical situation of the twenty-first century is different to that of the early twentieth century and aggression is simply not the answer. However, it is still pertinent to understand the relevance of Transfer of Technology (ToT) and Co-production from a foreign power. Being at a nascent stage in Defence Development and Production, India clearly needs friends who are willing to help it in its mission to achieve its goals of self- sufficiency. The idea is to be self-reliant in defence as quickly as possible and the good news is that with its new-found economic might and will, India might just have the bargaining power it so deserves. In a bid to prevent such fears (as faced by the Japanese during WW II) in the future, India aim for complete self-sufficiency in safeguarding percent its strategic interests. Indian defence budget is worth over $35 billion and is expected to grow by 17 percent in the financial year 2012-13; there are undoubtedly enormous trade volumes at India's disposal. In a recent report, Stockholm International Peace Research Institute (SIPRI) states that Indian defence spending rose 38 percent between 2007 and 2011 and India being the largest importer of arms took deliveries of almost 10 percent of all arms produced out of the total worth over $1.2 trillion destined for exports. Raking in the moolah that is being offered, Israel, like the Russians and the French, has been a major partner of India in not only defence but various other fields. The Indo-Israel Arms Trade is valued between $9 and 10 billion and is growing rapidly. Contributing to almost 50 percent of Israeli arms exports, India is definitely a significant partner; however, the most important part in this relationship is the fact that time and again Israel has emerged as reliable and dependable.

Partners such as Russia, France and Japan, and the emergence of Israel as a 'partner' (rather than a contractor) in defence, majorly started in 2004 with the $1.1 billion sale of ELM-2075 AEW radars for Indian Air Force's Russian IL 76 A-50 mounted AWAC (Airborne Early Warning and Control) system. Israel Aerospace Industries (IAI) and Elta Electronics Industry are major defence contractors engaged with India. Israel has been a key partner in the supply of equipment (with both Transfer of Technology and Co-production) and has been willing to aid India in developing self-sufficiency in sensitive technology not available for sale elsewhere. The Indo-Israeli partnership has been built on trust and support and withered various arms embargos by NATO members.

The SIPRI report makes it clear that India and other emerging countries spending big money on imports of defence equipment are doing so in order to develop their own indigenous military complexes. The case in point is the 30 percent plough back clause in any defence agreement India signs with a foreign partner; this clause makes it mandatory for any firm doing business with India to source 30 percent of the deal value from the Indian defence consortium. Even though the Indian military complex and defence infrastructure are mostly state-owned and comprise ordinance manufacturers, research and development laboratories, and eight Defense Public Sector Units, there are enormous cooperation opportunities in the near future. With a good track record, foreign firms should be encouraged to partner with close to 15 Raksha Udyog Ratna (RUR) Status Indian Private Sector Firms in developing weapon systems for the Indian armed forces. Keeping in mind the present mutual needs, partner nations can specially focus on space cooperation (Joint Development initiatives), Avionics, Unmanned Vehicles (UVs) and Jet Propulsion. Indian defence budget is expected to rise continuously for the next decade as India uses its monetary muscle to gain technologies for its self-reliant future, and Israel will be called upon as a friend and partner. For India, foreign partnerships may not simply be what America before 1941 was for Japan; a partner who turned hostile but a friend who stands by, come what may. As an inherent co-operator, India, according to analysts must understand its true allies. Concentrating their efforts, analysts believe that the Indo-Japan and Indo-Israeli partnerships have the potential to be as strong as the one between India and its all-weather friend Russia. With the present geopolitical climate, Israel, Japan and India face the same problems pertaining to global terrorism and regional volatility, and joint partnerships and co-production in defence are just the start of this symbiotic partnership between these three countries. Obviously, there is more to even today's high-tech war psyche than gambling; clearly there is a lot of thought involved here as well.

"If you want to learn about true nationalism then learn it from a fish, which dies as soon as it is taken out of its nation (water)."

—Subhash Chandra Bose,
Indian Freedom Fighter

The Psychology of a Ruthless (Inducted) Soldier

Ramah purastat partopi ramo ramah param dikshu vidikshu ramah |
Ramairanatairiti vishvarupo nighnannaratin virraj ramah ||

"Rama, the supreme being was everywhere, here, there, far, near, among the enemy and among the friends. Infinite Rama was omnipresent and there was no place left without him."

Powerful words if you understand the real relevance of the *Yudha Kanda* as war literature. *Ramayana*'s sixth *Kanda* among the seven *Kandas* (chronological books depicting the *Ramayana* epic) has been a major lesson in military strategy for years. Contrary to several translations, the literal Sanskrit translation signifies the idea of Lord Rama as a belief system. It illustrates the conviction of following the righteous way and the one established by god himself. On a different plane, the *Yudha Kanda* does not deliberately try to glorify God but the path set by him to be followed. It signifies the Vanara Sena's belief in the idea of Rama as a righteous leader and what he had set out to achieve, in short the winning of the Good over the Bad. The vanquishing of a well- equipped superior enemy at the hands of a smaller and somewhat ill- equipped Vanara Sena is a case in point here. The reason why the Lord Hanuman-led Vanara Sena reigned supreme in a battlefield deep inside enemy territory was the fact that the Sena was fighting as a collective unit bound by one common belief pertaining to righteousness. Therefore in essence, true to what is mentioned in the *Yudha Kanda*, this common belief system made every Vanara an *Avatara* of Rama and consequently becoming Rama himself. Seeing the ruthlessness and single-minded objectivity of the Sena, even the omnipotent enemy shuddered and envisioned its destruction and achieving *Nirvana* at the hands of the almighty Rama and his Avataras (Read: Vanara Sena). Under Lord Rama's name, the relatively insignificant, in number, Vanara Sena successfully fought against Ravana's 36,000 mighty *Akshouhini* battle formations (each battle formation consisting of 1,09,350 soldiers, 21,870 elephants, 65,610 horse riders and 21,870 battle chariots led by one *Maharathi* [Centurion Commander]).

Even in modern warfare, there are several instances sighting examples when small armies have defeated seemingly invincible foes. Among prominent ones, the 1973 Yom Kippur War (popularly known as the Six Day War) is a prime example that throws light on the subject of Central Belief System pertaining to a soldier. It was not very different when Israeli Armed Forces successfully fought against the combined might of 13 Arab Nations clandestinely supported by Cuba and North Korea. With its meagre 200,000 (estimated) foot soldiers, Israel successfully regained its lost position in North Africa (in and around the Suez Canal) within 6 days and was relentlessly progressing even further into Arab territories before ceasefire. Israel's convincing win established the fact that Israel (often termed insignificant) was the most potent military power in the entire Middle East/North Africa/West Asia region. The main reason why Israel with its 200,000 soldiers, 1700 tanks and 400 fighter aircrafts defeated an Arab army consisting of an estimated1,000,000 soldiers (5:1 ratio), 3500 tanks, 300 navy vessels and over 1000 fighter aircrafts was simple, Israel had no second option. An Israeli soldier's belief system was connected to the fear of losing his home. In the wake of an Arab strike on Israel, the country's soldier found himself/herself in a position where he/she was inherently risking his/her home, family and a sense of belonging if the War had been lost. Thus, the well-documented bravado of an Israeli soldier during the war was connected to the fear of annihilation and winning was the only option (the famous *Burning Bridges Tactic*).

Another example is the 1904 Russo-Japanese War, when Japan, a relatively unknown global player, decisively defeated the mighty and undefeated Russian Empire militarily. The War, which led to a Japanese acquisition of Korea, Greater Manchuria and then claims to large swathes of Greater China, established Japan as a world power, tilting the balance of power in the East in its favour. At the end of the War, the victory of the Imperial Japanese military had resulted in (killed, wounded during the war and post-war diseases) the deaths of close to half of the 500,000 Russian soldiers engaged in that particular battle. The legendary Japanese ruthlessness was again directly bound by a belief system that was connected to the establishment of Japan as a World Power post the Meiji Restoration. Japan's military was a cohesive, well-organised unit driven by a desire to establish its supremacy and a desire for world recognition (at least that is what they thought).

After its humiliating defeat in the 1971 Bangladesh Liberation War, the Pakistani army believed that it could increase the chances of winning a war by instilling collective ruthlessness among its soldiers, through the inclusion of the Jihad concept in the country's military doctrine. Reportedly, special lessons were arranged during routine trainings of the military and soldiers were programmed to be religious soldiers rather than national. Even though, this strategy more or less backfired due to an increasing hardliner presence in the Pakistani army, resulting in the country's prevailing 'identity crisis,' the strategy paid off as it made the Pakistani army less jittery when faced by constant fears concerning India's overwhelming capabilities, keeping India's alleged 'backyardism' in the SAARC region in check.

Not a popular example, but during the 1939-45 World War II, the Nazi Army, under the Third Reich was an invincible force. Even though, the *Wehrmacht* (the Nazi military) was relatively small and had a limited number of soldiers under its command, it was trying to fight a three-pronged war against an army three times its size, sometimes effectively so. With such ambitions, there must have been a very strong belief system among the Nazi-controlled military that it could actually achieve its goals, even if it meant fighting the entire world for it. Obviously, the Nazis were fighting for a cause that can at best be described inhuman; the psychological cohesiveness achieved by their military was certainly outstanding nonetheless because there was determination to win at all costs. While the Nazi central belief system was connected to the Aryan supremacy dogma, the

Wehrmacht was a ruthless, cohesive and a highly effective force with a clear chain of command in most cases.

In all sanity, a soldier must be humane and abide by human values as the primary directive of being part of a military force. However, I believe that a military's effectiveness and chances of winning directly depends upon its Central Belief System (collective or unified thought) that binds it cohesively. Only a belief that is original, effectively communicated and appeals to a country's citizens can achieve a Cohesive Military Might. After analysing several examples from around the world and our own literatures, it is clear that winning a war is not directly proportional to a quantitative advantage but a qualitative advantage. I have specially emphasised on the word 'ruthlessness' because I believe that the word effectively measures a soldier's appetite to win wars at all costs. As a result, a war is not simply a period during which a soldier lives or dies; it is a conflict of beliefs. **The side which has the stronger Belief System is more agile, cohesive and adaptable and ultimately wins**. Military might may not be the last and the only option for achieving greatness but a well-established/all-engulfing doctrine defines who we are militarily, socially and economically, because ultimately this cohesiveness percolates into everything that we do as a Collective and as its people. Therefore, to be an effective fighting machine, a soldier must be an embodiment of the belief system that he/she shares with his/her side and strive to perform his/her *Dharma*, come what may.

As rightly pointed out by Lord Krishna to a subdued and lost Arjuna during the Battle of *Mahabharata*:

> *Atha cet tvam imam dharmyam sangramam na karisyasi tatahsva-dharmam kirtim ca hitva papam avapsyasi* ||
>
> "If you do not perform your *Dharma* to fight, you will certainly sustain sins for abandoning your duties and reputation as a soldier (fighter)."

The Power of Propaganda

Not so long ago, hard-hitting masculine *Rambo* series came out of Hollywood. It was one of those movie series that inspired an entire generation and accurately ensconced American heroism into everyday public psyche. Like all American war hero movies, *Rambo* series was a mass influencer of public sentiment of those days. The lean mean killing machine Sylvester Stallone was an embodiment of the ultimate national hero and was presented as a messiah of the downtrodden. So when this American hero fought against the Soviets, he supported the 'depicted' ill-equipped but brave Afghan Mujahidin rebels and helped liberate the latter. Almost two decades later, when another American hero Robert Downey Jr., in the *Iron Man* movie series, massacred the Taliban (read erstwhile Mujahidin), history came a full circle. The dramatic turn of events baffles an ardent follower of Hollywood and American Heroism. Seeing the contradiction I could not help but wonder—on whose side does the American legion lie anyway? I simply adore the uncanny ability of America (through Hollywood) to be on the side of the perceived good guys of the world. Apparently American heroes have no qualms in trading sides as and when the geopolitical situation changes. The up-to-date ardency of America through its movies has an underlying motive to represent American interests in the best possible way and showcase how much the nation cares about the world. Human memory is short lived, but a well-rehearsed propaganda can sure be a lethal combination, given Hollywood's influence.

Personally I do not have any reservations against American military and economic might as it is well earned. In all sanity America is the sole superpower of a unipolar world and it has attained the position through the resilience of its people. However, I believe that there are some ingenious examples which America has used very cleverly to its advantage in order to project its collective might and can be dissected to gain valuable insights. After a major setback in the Vietnam War, America has mastered the art of conflict negotiations through eminence without direct military engagements.

The American deployment of aircraft carriers (Enterprise class and, more recently, Nimitz class) as propaganda prior to negotiations is an example of non-violent conflict resolution employed solely for negotiations. In recent time, their role was apparent in the

Persian Gulf, East China Sea/Taiwanese Strait and the Yellow Sea. It should be noted that the positioning of the American aircraft carriers influences the outcome of negotiations engaged by America in any part of the world. During the Indo-Pakistan War of 1971, the position of USS Enterprise (Seventh Fleet) in the Bay of Bengal before the US negotiated with India on the behest of Pakistan is a prime example. Also, during the Arab–Israel conflict, American aircraft carriers continued to patrol the Persian Gulf, Gulf of Aden and were stationed at the Indian Ocean Island base, Diego Garcia almost permanently giving a clear message to Egypt and her Arab allies. Before the first Gulf war too, the position of a Nimitz class carrier (and its accompanying fleet) in the Persian Gulf imposed terms on the Saddam-led Iraqi regime—'leave Kuwait or else'—even before the war actually started. Even though the war did take place and the American aircraft carriers did play an important role; the importance of a carrier as a 'scarecrow' was still more than evident. While I do not doubt the capabilities of these 100,000 tonne beasts, but I do believe in their usage as 'negotiators' rather than military 'enforcers'. The Chairman of the National Maritime Foundation, Admiral (Retd.) Arun Prakash states in his prologue for the book, *The Aircraft Carrier in the 21st Century*, "The Korea War, The Suez Canal crises, The Vietnam War and the Falklands Campaign are just some examples in which carriers made a significant contribution—quite apart from hundreds of "hot spots" or potential conflict scenarios where the presence of a carrier task force has defused the situation."

Rightly so, it's almost like putting a gun on the table before the start of an argument—well aware of the fact that the other party is already aware of the outcome. This is the point at which Hollywood enters. American movies have used this showcase of power and might in the depiction of American aircraft carriers as the echelons of power, controlling the high seas and hence the world. The physical American blue water capability is thus augmented by Hollywood creating a semblance of power and communicating in advance what exactly America wants (when it sends its ships). The erstwhile Northrop Grumman F-14 Tomcats roaring and conquering the skies taking off from force multiplier aircraft carrier platforms in movies such as 1985's *Top Gun* is a case in point. Of course as predicted, in most cases, such movies end with America winning the war against the evil, liberating the world; the most important point here is the 'depiction' that America almost never loses a war and never leaves its 'friends' at the mercy of a predator.

Showcasing of advance but unavailable technology in Hollywood is yet another case of outrageous propaganda. Several cases of technology demonstrator platforms that are nothing more than figments of imagination have not only made Hollywood movies heavy on special effects but have also given America an imaginary technology edge. America is able to demonstrate its might through the movies while preserving an aura of mystery through the Hollywood concoction of secrecy and power projection. The world in general (which knows America largely through its movies) believes that American capabilities are beyond comprehension and that the country has deep wells of secret technology which has never been unleashed—a belief that when mixed with physical military presence becomes believable and, of course, lethal; Area 51* anyone? With an equal, if not a better, medium, India can take valuable lessons from America's Hollywood. Bollywood (I personally do not promote this moniker though), perhaps churning out more movies than Hollywood, has helped project India's soft power and can be a more potent medium. Several policy experts believe that the Pakistani propaganda behind the Kashmir crisis and the Khalistan movement was much more successful than the subsequent Indian military interventions. The greatest error made by Indian films is that they continue to portray Indian discontent with the government's failure to take such issues seriously. Most movies, such as the 2003's *Zameen* and *A Wednesday*, were brilliantly directed movies but were nothing more than 'frustration pacifiers'. Indian cinema should ideally show India in a new light as a power that exists and should not dwell in the 'what should have been scenario'. The rich Indian culture and the very popular Indian cuisine has already established India as an admired country; Bollywood simply has to chip in to take things a little forward.

To make matters easier, Indian armed forces possess almost all necessary equipment to be part of an action-packed Bollywood backdrop. The 5th generation fighter jets, aircraft carriers, nuclear submarines, top notch navy commandos, space technology and even potentially advanced technology developments (could be duds or speculations but who cares?) are all there to be exploited. Even though there may not be numerous defence contractors such as Northrop Grumman, Lockheed Martin and Boeing (McDonnell Douglas) located in this country but India's public defence consortium consisting of DRDO, Cochin Shipyard and HAL is sufficient to form a covert operation for an advanced technology backdrop for any Bollywood thriller. You see the idea is to develop and present a 'perception' which is believable and if not globally, regionally acceptable. When people say that India should not waste money on demonstrators such as unmanned Moon missions and Mars missions, space-manned missions, scramjet engines and other advanced technology platforms they should understand that even if these technologies eventually fail (or the money spent could be used in better ways) the basic idea is to establish a reasonable halo effect around our capabilities. I believe that this is the new power projection of the twenty-first century. For India Collective to survive and for the revival of its self- confidence, this is just one of the power projections this country might have to do out of several. In the global scheme of things, certainly, we have a role to play here because, remember, we are the Good Guys.

"It always feels impossible until it is done."

—Nelson Mandela

Past, Future and Present

"Sadbhavana demands 'Sauna Saath, Sauna Vikas', meaning inclusive growth with collective efforts"
"It is an apolitical social movement to spread the message of peace and harmony from Gujarat to showcase to the world"

—Narendra Modi, Patan,
Gujarat (2011)

After taking the oath of office as the 15th Prime Minister of India, Narendra Modi in his first speech to the Parliament's Upper House time and again mentioned about his concept of 'Cooperative Federalism' and why it is important. As per Modi, without a collective effort, there cannot be a meaningful development of India and that all states must work together with the centre for maximum performance and good of the people. There is a lot of truth in Narendra Modi's belief system as it is directly linked with India's formation as a Collective. Since Collectivisation is the primary crux of this thinking, Cooperatisation of India is the next logical conclusion for the country's socio-economic evolution.

In all probability, Modi's association with collaboration and collectivity has brought him directly in line with the concepts of Swaraj and self-reliance, concepts which were already incorporated into the India Collective thousands of years ago. Earlier, the mass appeal generated by Kejriwal, resurrected the aforementioned concept making it the central pillar of India's revival as a value system. With India's new PM firmly backing these values, it's heartening to note how the assimilative powers of the India Collective spawns seemingly lost stimuli and presents in another time frame as if they were never lost in oblivion. In instances like these, India showcases its true powers and appropriately positions itself in three dimensions effectively communicating what it truly represents—The India Collective.

"Vasudhaiva Kutumbakam, it's in our DNA"

—Narendra Modi

In all probability, India's second renaissance must start at the grass-root level with people from all walks of life coming together and building a country that they and their progeny will be proud of. In twenty-first century India, collectivity is back with a bang and resurrected through collective action by civil society after the dastardly Delhi gangrape of 2013. Prominent figures such as Anna Hazare and Arvind Kejriwal further perfected this collectivity through their revival plan of 'Swaraj' as a concept and finally current Indian Prime Minister Narendra Modi, who envisions a new India built on these values. Delhi Chief Minister Kejriwal is right when he says that India's policy frameworks must emanate from the local level: RWAs in the urban centres and Gram Panchayats at the rural—just as the India Collective has been represented in its glorious past.

From the Vanara Sena's single-minded objectivity to defend truth from evil to the ancient Vaishali kingdom's attempted collective action towards collective good (Kejriwal's interpretation); from Jamsetji Tata's collective mobilisation of Indian citizenry in order to build modern India's backbone to Mahatma Gandhi's Dandi March; from Mumbai's women entrepreneurs uniting to form one of the world's most influential all-women organisations to Gujarati milk-sellers coming together to set up modern India's most powerful dairy brand—Collectivity is at the core of it all.

Modern India has now identified its core value system as cooperation, and it is now overwhelmingly showing itself in all facets of Indian day-to-day life. As collectivity showcases itself again, India is apparently reliving a history, though long forgotten, resurrecting itself with full splendour. It seems this country is alive and reorganising itself with each new phase of its evolution; adapting and presenting a hybrid that is never the same but represents what it is truly meant to be in terms of its core values.

> *"Bharat ek jeet jagta rashtra purush"*
>
> —Atal Bihvari Vajpayee

"Ubuntu: 'I' am because 'We' are."

—African Tribe Philosophy

Case Study 1

Cooperation is the Beginning of Swaraj

> *"Holistic and accelerated development of compact areas around a potential growth centre in a Gram Panchayat (or a group of GPs) through Public Private Partnership (PPP) framework for providing livelihood opportunities and urban amenities to improve the quality of life in Rural Areas."*

In January 2003, the then President of India, Dr. A.P.J. Abdul Kalam discussed his concept of PURA or Provision of Urban Amenities in Rural Areas. Dr. Kalam and co-author Srijan Pal Singh had vehemently analysed this RurbaniSation model in their book, Target 3 Billion, and believed that India needs to provide urban facilities in its rural areas if it aspires to be a developed country and provide meaningful socio-economic subsistence to its people. The then Prime Minister Vajpayee was instrumental in the implementation of this vision and a pilot in select Indian states was formally launched in the year 2004. Even though PURA was put on hold when the NDA lost power and its concept was superseded by other populist schemes, it was however resurrected by Jairam Ramesh, the UPA's then Rural Development Minister of India, albeit in a considerably tweaked and restructured format. The pilot now focuses more on 'connected infrastructure' rather than 'connected minds' (as envisioned by Kalam).

The PURA model[21] is simple as it focuses on building usable infrastructure in rural areas in order to provide sustainable and dignified livelihood to the local citizens. As a business model, the pilot identifies a Gram Panchayat or a group of GPs with a population of about 40,000 people and calls the area a project site. After detailed viability and baseline studies a private sector partner is identified and work in the creation of rural infrastructure and services is initiated with funding provisions through MoRD, private sources and PURA grants. Currently, the following are the main focal areas of the scheme:

- Village Street Lighting
- Electricity Generation
- Integrated Rural Hub & Market
- Skill Development & Economic Ability Creation
- Common Service Centres & Warehousing
- Telecommunication
- Waste Management & Sewerage

Even before he became India's Finance Minister, Arun Jaitley (late), senior politician and one of the BJP's frontmen suggested that his party's manifesto will not totally dismantle the populist schemes set up by the UPA Government but will focus on 'Real Asset Creation.' He said:

> *"BJP's economic model should encourage entrepreneurship. However, considering the large scale poverty in India, we cannot merely depend on the economic growth to pull people out of poverty. Poverty alleviation schemes are necessary. The schemes, however, have to also be linked to asset creation."*[22]

It seems overwhelmingly plausible that the PURA model of development is back in action and the present government will focus on the scheme and its vision vehemently. Surprisingly, this is also similar to the Gujarat model of development, where Prime Minister Narendra Modi swears by his 'Rurbanisation 50' model in Gujarat. Under this model, the Gujarat Government has identified 50 villages in the state and initiated a process of upgradation of infrastructure such as roads, schools and hospitals. Modi, who launched this scheme in Gujarat in the year 2011, believed that upgrading the village infrastructure would not only stop unsolicited migration but also create sustainable livelihoods and promote the idea of 'Swaraj' or self-governance. The BJP (and NDA) envision a more decentralised governance and apparently, the PURA model of Rurbanisation is the answer to its vision of self-governance through public–private partnerships.

The Planning Commission of India, on its part has been pushing the Rurbanisation model over the last two Five Year Plans. The 11th Plan strongly fostered the formation of Self Help Groups (SHGs) and community empowerment, and the now-famous Aajiveeka scheme[23] under the National Rural Livelihood Mission (MoRD) was implemented to promote sustainable rural development. The project aims to cover 2.5 lakh Panchayats comprising 600 districts and 70 million rural poor households by organising them in village SHGs that are economically viable and productive. The 12th Plan went one step ahead and introduced other sustainability models with a special focus on 'Renewable Energy' for rural empowerment. The Commission for example, wants to more than double the installed capacity of renewable energy from 24 GW in 2014 to 55 GW by the end of the 12th Five Year plan period and envisions the incorporation of numerous examples of off-grid and community-driven energy initiatives.

Even the much hyped Mahatma Gandhi National Rural Employment Guarantee Act (MGNREGA) scheme, which had mandated a 60:40 funding ratio—symbolising the fact that 60 percent of all allocation for the scheme will go in wage payment while the rest will be spent on asset creation or allied services—is also on the verge of change with a clearer focus on 'permanent asset creation and its maintenance' through local rural communities. It seems that MGNREGA is now converging with other central government funded schemes for maximum impact and community participation.

Therefore, it is now apparent that India is heading towards a convergence development mechanism that will base itself on cooperation and collective action. With this regard, I could not help but correlate this return to convergence phenomenon with South Korea's acclaimed Saemaul Undong (New Village) Movement, which started in the year 1972. It is one of the most pioneering examples of cooperatisation and community-enabled asset creation, and it relates with A.P.J. Abdul Kalam's PURA concept. You see, both these concepts can be related to each other because they talk about how communities can help themselves through collective action, and I think there is a great correlation in what they both set out to achieve.

The best aspect of the South Korean movement, in my opinion, was its emphasis on morality and harmony, as demonstrated by the following:

- Mentality—Better relationship with neighbours
- Behavorial/Action—Manners and public conduct
- Environmental—Cleanliness and sustainable development

The Saemaul Movement was so successful that by the movement's 3rd year of existence, conclusive results were apparent and South Korea's 35,000 villages were divided under three areas pertaining to Underdeveloped, Self Help and Self-Reliant based on performances. Within a short span of time, over 98 percent of villages became economically independent and rural incomes soon overtook even urban incomes. Astounding as it may sound, the way the movement worked was simple: villages were provided 335 sacks of cement and expected to use the resource to build their local infrastructure through collective action; if the performance was found to be good, an additional 500 sacks of cement and a tonne steel rods were sanctioned as a reward. This system created a competitive environment and village communities competed for the best 'rewards' available from the state; this resulted in an extremely conducive environment for development based on cooperative self-help of the communities.

Just like the present thought processes in India, then PresidentPark Chung Hee believed that merely doling out government funds to people would eventually be useless in developing the desperately poor communities; according to him, nothing notable can be achieved without communities themselves taking part in their socio-economic upliftment. The underlying idea of this Saemaul Movement was the 'creation of oneness in the society' and 'laying down the foundation for peaceful coexistence'.

Three Guiding Spirits:

- Diligence
- Self Help
- Cooperation/Two hands are better than one

The goal of the movement simply put was building a united community and then a united nation, restoring peace and order. Community projects were need-based and community-driven, where people had direct control over what and where to develop, resulting in full democratic control over planning and work. Regarding my concerns over India's IBIN lacking government support (stated earlier), in South Korea as a contrast, the Ministry of Internal Affairs as well as other ministries were actively involved in the Saemaul Movement, which was effectively manoeuvred by the state.

Convergence of the MGNREGA, PURA and Saemual Movement

As I mentioned earlier, it seems plausible that India combines the best qualities of the MGNREGA and PURA model with the Saemaul Movement of sustainable development. As with everything else, a collective might of all three concepts will herald a new method of grassroot level development in India and will benefit millions of Indians. As explained earlier in the chapter concerning the

Metropolitan Regions, such arrangement will transcend the Rural and Urban divide and will represent a 'Region under Management' approach—where both rural and urban centres will collectively function as components of a larger area for the collective good of all stakeholders.

Examining the MGNREGA scheme, in 2014, the annual allocation for the scheme is Rs. 35,000 crore spread over close to 44 million people. As on 2022-23, the allocations have remained near that level. A quick maths reveals that the scheme was able to provide Rs. 8,000 per person annually. Even if it covers around 6,00,000 villages with a population of close to 720 million people, the scheme is capable of providing employment for 41 days (rather than 100 days) on average—it can be assumed that each covered individual got Rs. 195 daily.

Working Together Orientation

MGNREGA ALLOCATION PREDICTION MODEL											
Year	2012	2013	2014	2015	2016	2017	2018	2019	2020	2021	2022
Eligible Population (in crore)	4.28	4.32708	4.37467788	4.422799337	4.47145	4.520636	4.570363	4.620637	4.671464	4.72285	4.774802
Fiscal Budget (100 days wage for Eligible) Rupee Crore	85600	86541.6	87493.5576	88455.98673	89429	90412.72	91407.26	92412.74	93429.28	94457	95496.03
Fiscal Budget (100 days wage for Eligible) Euro Million	10176	10287.94	10401.1033	10515.51543	10631.19	10748.13	10866.36	10985.89	11106.73	11228.91	11352.43
Fiscal Budget (Current 41 days wage for Eligible) Rupee Crore	35000	35385	35774.235	36167.75159	36565.6	36967.82	37374.46	37785.58	38201.22	38621.44	39046.27
Fiscal Budget (Current 41 days wage for Eligible) Euro Million	4160	4205.76	4252.02336	4298.795617	4346.082	4393.889	4442.222	4491.086	4540.488	4590.434	4640.929
%age Increase in Eligible Population (If Rural Casual Labour Ra	1%										
180860.4019											
215860.4019				5 Year Period (12th Plan)							
			Required Budget (Eur	52583.86998							
442332.8685			Actual Budget (Euro M	21496.55062							
			Actual Eligible Families (with average 6 members, including 2 of working age)								
				21.4 Million							

With such a budget at its disposal, it is clear that this government-funded scheme places an immense firepower in the hands of the poor.

As mentioned earlier in this book, the current BJP Government is keen on converting the scheme into a more productive avenue for the creation of permanent assets. What if the MGNREGA scheme is reoriented to fund community self-help from the current centrally administered 'money for free scheme'? How about an outlook that is tweaked towards collective action and development that is a community prerogative? What if, MGNREGA is modified as a modern version of South Korea's 'New Village Movement', but in our case is not specifically rural-oriented? Communities can be provided with building material that is valued at the money allocated to each individual as per the MGNREGA scheme. If every person through the scheme gets Rs. 8000, then a family of 5 may receive building materials worth Rs. 16000 every year (considering 2 members, who are eligible). In such a scenario, a village community of 5000 people, can raise an annual Rs. 1.6 crore for building durable infrastructure for themselves and their progeny! The communities can autonomously decide where and how they would like to use their money, whether it is for building schools, small manufacturing entities, community hospitals, solar power, off-grid energy solutions or community housing projects. As India becomes wealthier and the government is able to raise more money through direct and indirect taxes and other sources of revenue there can be more cash replenishments for the self-help communities. This could lead to a PURA type model of development envisioned by former Indian President A.P.J. Abdul Kalam and Srijan Pal Singh. The only difference that the redesigned model will include not only private effort but also public funding, resulting in a true Public Private Partnership. Swaraj's actual powers will be revealed, and the Indian people will come to understand their collective and what it is capable of. This model can be retrofitted into the Metropolitan Region concept that has been suggested by this book elsewhere. Collective action at the rural level will incorporate larger populations into its fold, with villages themselves eventually becoming higher order centres (in a regional context) evolving into central sustainers of a larger diaspora.

Case Study 2

Sugar Commons

If you travel through the Indian hinterlands during the *ganna* season—a time when sugarcane is harvested and sold to sugar mills—there is absolutely no escaping from the chaos that ensues. Roads are clogged with hundreds or even thousands of bullock carts, tractor trailers and trucks loaded with sugarcane to the hilt—slowly plodding along the otherwise swift traffic (comparatively!). There is so much activity on the roads during these times that resultant traffic jams, chaos and bagasse create a feel that lingers even after you cross over. Not without reason, this immense economic activity creates Rs. 39,000 crore annually for the farmers while contributing Rs. 2,200 crore to central and Rs. 1,100 crore to state exchequers.

For a closer look at what the sugar industry means to India, consider the following facts as per the Indian Institute of Sugarcane Research (IISR), Lucknow, *Vision 2030* document:

- 6 million farmers depend on sugarcane for livelihood
- Current area under sugarcane is 4.4 million hectares
- Current average productivity is 68 tonnes per hectare
- Currently there are 490 sugar mills processing the crop
- Currently, the country produced 18.9 million tonnes of sugar, which is 11.8 percent of the world production
- Being water-intensive, nearly 200-250 tonnes of water is required for the production of 1 tonne of sugar
- Sugarcane consumes 6.46 percent of the country's irrigation potential while occupying only 2.55 percent of India's net cultivated area

- Being labour-intensive, sugarcane requires 250-400 man days per hectare: 50 percent of the cost is labour cost
- 50 percent of the total area under sugarcane is between 0.5–5 hectares; 20.7 percent of the area is between 5-10 hectares

Furthermore, the KPMG Report, *The Indian Sugar Industry (Sector Report 2017)*, mentions the following:

> *"The landholding size of 4 hectares or more is present in only 25% of the area under sugarcane cultivation. The bulk of the land under sugarcane is between 1 and 4 hectares. This land holding structure is a key structural feature of the sugar industry in India. There are more than 50 million farmers and families involved in the sugarcane cultivation and these farmers supply sugarcane to almost 500 mills in various parts of the nine sugar producing states. Therefore, on an average, each mill procures cane from 18000 farmers, which is one the highest in the world."*

Strangely, despite the big numbers and apparent importance in global terms, India's sugar industry spreads only $6.5 billion among those whose lives depend on it—close to 6 million of them. In Brazil, a fellow BRIC nation which is the world's largest producer of sugar, nearly $8 billion are spread among 1 million people depending on it for subsistence (if we do not account the huge sugar energy sector that accounts for much more). In the US, which is a developed country having no direct economic correlation to India, nearly $1 billion[1] are spread among just 14,000 people!

Again using simple algebra, we obtain the average salary (per capita) of agricultural workers in these three relatively distinct countries:

- Indian Farmer: $1,100
- Brazilian Farmer: $8,000 (not incorporating energy sub sector)
- United States Farmer: $65,000 (not incorporating sugarbeet and energy sub sector)

Even if per capita income of an Indian farmer is calculated in terms of the Purchasing Power Parity (PPP) approach, the average income is no more than $3,500!

High population dependency is obviously not at fault here because Indian agriculture has not stabilised yet. As per IISR data, by the year 2030, the area under sugarcane will stabilise at 5 million hectares and productivity will increase to 100-110 tonnes/hectare from current 68 tonnes/hectare levels. It is further estimated by other experts that India has hardly used its status as a major sugarcane cultivating country when it comes to influencing global prices and commodity markets. With 15 percent of the global sugar demand being met by India, the country should have ideally consolidated this industry into the global supply chain more efficiently and into the many sub-sectors that have resulted. KPMG estimates that India had the potential to export 10 MMT of sugar by the year 2017 as compared to 2014 levels of just 2 MMT. This figure has been achieved, as on 2021-22.

Brazil's sugarcane industry, for example, derives only a quarter of the wealth created from sugar production while the rest comes from the sugar energy production. In the Latin American economic powerhouse, nearly 50 percent of all sugarcane cultivation is exclusively reserved for the energy sector. Ethanol, which is derived from processing sugarcane, has become one of the major sources of revenue for Brazil so much so that the country exports billions of dollars worth of ethanol every year. Since Brazil has been facing major inflationary pressures for several decades, the country's dependence on expensive petroleum products has also significantly subsided given the country's usage of ethanol instead—today over 90 percent of cars sold in that country are ethanol-ready. This bifurcation not only made the country environmentally sustainable, but also initiated a revolution that that resulted in unprecedented wealth creation in Brazil—catapulting it to become Latin America's wealthiest country and one of the world's most innovative countries.

In India, nearly 80 percent of sugarcane is utilised in the manufacture of sugar or *gur*, which not only lowers profitability but also leaves very little to add to substantial value through diversification. The Government of India is sceptical towards using sugarcane as an energy resource as that might lead to a situation where farmers will be tempted to replace food security crops with the former, leading to a chronic food shortage. Given that the worldwide ethanol market is projected to grow to 150 billion litres in the next decade, up from the present 10 billion litres, I beg to differ. My argument that the problem is not with the perceived repercussions of granting a 'Cash Crop Status', but with an inability to efficiently manage the harvest due to small landholdings and individual farmer isolation.

It is all about forming collectives among sugarcane farmers and educating them about the potential value generation they can access if they work together. If farmers with small landholdings come together, they can not only increase their bargaining power, but also be effectively managed by Government segregation policies concerning sugar and energy utilisation of the crop. Also, cooperatives can be controlled through effectively enforcing 'area under sugarcane' limits, which leads to an increase in efficiencies and modernisations and helps farmers in dealing with mechanisation and capital intensiveness.

Deriving from this logic, if 50 percent of the 18,000 farmers (having landholdings between 0.5–5 hectares) in every milling area cooperatise themselves, then we might have every area represented by a 9,000-member collective farm output. Think of the economy of scale in production, planning, financial pooling and trading power of this collective unit. Think of the financial muscle these cooperatives will enjoy that will give them the power to bargain for their rights and affirmatively plan for their future development, including incorporation of new methods and own processing and branding units. America's Sugarcane Growers Cooperative of Florida is a great example to consider and compare. With such volumes, the Indian sugarcane industry will never be the same: cooperation will not only bring organisation but also a massive push towards collective wealth creation and welfare to the marginalised.

One possible approach would be for collectives to own or at the very least govern their mills. Even though nearly half of all sugar mills in India are known as cooperatives, it is evident that they are far from cooperative. Most are started by the government's seed capital and are now owned and managed by influential farmers and businessmen leaving out the marginal farmers. The Mahajan Committee[2] has recommended that the cooperative sugar mills should shed their government funding and dependence and transform into true cooperative enterprises, with their own prerogative in managing their finances, ownership and R&D. However, this has fallen on deaf ears and recommendations have gone unnoticed.

In the present age of global completion, mere Government-induced Minimum Support Price (MSP) mechanisms will not suffice in improving productivity and ushering wealth creation as per the potential. Farmers must come together and create wealth for themselves by being active free market players and compete for wealth. The Government of India might continue its subsidy support like its American and Brazilian counterparts and allow the industry to mature at its own pace. While this is easier said than done, it is now up to the India Collective to seize control and usher in a Sugar Revolution.

Notes

1. Economic Research Service, US Department of Agriculture, http://www.ers.usda.gov/topics/crops/sugar-sweeteners/background.aspx#.U_20pfmSyFU (2013/14)
2. KPMG India: The Indian Sugar Industry- Sector Roadmap 2017 (June 2007)

A Simple Truth...

After putting in much effort and failing to understand intellectual blasphemies, I realised that influencing mass opinion did not really require arcane numbers and history lessons. For once, the world really does not need personal opinions to become civilised overnight. Looking at things around us, it does not take much time in figuring out the fact that an opinion's success rate depends on its ability to percolate and seep into the social hierarchies. If an opinion is founded on facts and data that appeal to the target audience's academic allegiances, it is certain to remain specialised and unproven. If you examine any 'significant' revolution around the world, you will notice that the basic notion is usually always quite simple and just does its job well (that is hitting the nail on the head). As an example, there was nothing profoundly intellectual about the Arab Spring, which transformed much of North Africa. It started with a simple idea in Tunisia that an oppressive government must go. What started was a mass movement against oppressive governments in the entire region, which spread even beyond North Africa into Syria.

Therefore, in essence the idea was really very simple as it took into account a very popular mass opinion. In India, Mahatma Gandhi's Quit India Movement was so successful because during that epoch it called upon a very common ambition of Indians at large—independence from British Rule. The recent Anna Hazare-led Anti-Corruption Movement is another case in point here. The rise of 'India against Corruption' simply rides on a brand of morality that people are willing to accept today for a better India. There was really nothing particularly intellectual about the idea of Anti-Corruption, as it is a menace everybody is aware of and detests. The only reason why this opinion took engulfing proportions was due to the fact that everybody could relate to it from day one: simple. Even though a lot of agitators from the general public had no idea (and they still don't) as to what actually Anti-Corruption Bill was really all about and what merits it would bring, the best part was that everybody could convincingly buy the argument. While it may be the worst thing that can happen to a stock market, but the concept of *Herd Mentality* as it is called, is not always a bad thing. You see the idea is to amplify the ripple effect of an opinion that has the power to make life significantly better, for all (and as mentioned earlier, our *chai* stalls are called for active duty!). The amplifier that I am talking about is simplicity, and that is what this book is all about (you may disagree!).

Getting back to the book's main business, I have deliberately followed a reporting-style milieu for this book with a concoction of opinions, statistics and insights. You may ask why? Well, my primary reason to write this book is not to establish my point of view or represent the journalist community's agony, but to celebrate the idea of simplicity of thought. It is critical for you, the reader, to understand not just what I have to say, but also what the most important people have to say to you. I have tried to be a medium and, therefore, there is a synthesis of thoughts doing the rounds here. While following the central idea of simplicity, I have written this book with quotes from the people who I believe can make a difference to our lives while incorporating my own 'oh so sacrosanct' views (which you may ignore completely). For those of you who are a little sceptical and are stuck with this book (or are just luckily reading this part)—'What's with Simplicity?' You might ask. I have my reasons.

For starters, I started my career as a journalist. I am sure most journalists will agree with me when I say that journalists are the biggest recyclers (read: simplifiers) of information in the whole wide world. Given the fact that our salaries are inversely proportional to our abilities, we are a rare breed of hacks, who delve into the most complex information for you and present a creation that you as a reader understands without frantically consulting the encyclopaedia every morning. So, in essence we not only destroy the encyclopaedia market (so much so that they are actually moving online), which is so tastefully developed by our thought leaders, but also make the world a lot simpler place to live in (or just be). The idea of this book started with a routine 'thinking man' session, after witnessing a collectivity in motion without prejudice. I realised that the number one reason for people not working together is miscommunication and ambiguity. Often, we realise that we could have acted or thought differently to avert things from going wrong—if only we could work together and act differently if we knew how. It's almost always that we crave for this elusive right way (a simple one-step solution) to follow when we are in a deep mess.

With this book, it's not that I am looking to change our country just because I had a sudden "eureka" moment while pretending to be standing on a moral high ground, rather, I have come to believe that simplicity of thought is not limited to social cohesions alone; simplicity of thought, I believe, is almost like the brain's dopamine hormone, aiding neuron transmissions effectively. It is about time that intellectuals realise the fact that influencing a certain social segment does not bring about desired results and that such opinions fail to generate the envisaged ripples. We as a nation have had enough of perspectives; what we really need is information that we can use to make our lives better. For a variety of reasons, none of us has time to contemplate the complexities of politics and business; all we need is a mechanism to determine what is best for us and some assurance that those who make decisions are aware of our concerns. In this book, I have tried to present a framework of opinions that, when combined into a 'single concept,' has the potential to revolutionise our society for the better. I have always believed that if we as a society have access to information that is relevant yet simple to comprehend and follow we all can see to make our lives better (irrespective of our socio-economic backgrounds).

Ultimately, it is us who make the citizenry, government, heroes, intellectuals and the bureaucrats of this country. All we need is the correct direction to guide our collective energies toward achieving our goals in our own unique way. This book is our campaign for India.

As a country, we are capable of taking collective actions, as we always have done in the past. Our collective solidarity during tough times is proof of this. Why I ask, can't we be a Collective for everything we do as a nation? This is because our collectivity, , truly represents who we are as a civil society. We only need a fresh intent and nothing else to be a successful country and a global leader 'again'.

Notes

1. Vincent A. Smith, *The Early History of India* Available online at http://books.google. (2013/14) (Publisher: Elite Agencies) co.in/books?id=8XXGhAL1WKcC&pg=PA322&lpg=PA322&dq=The+-foreigners,+like+their+forerunners+the+Sakas+and+the+Yueh-chi,+universally+yielded+to+the+wonder ful+assimilative+powers+of+Hinduism,+and+rapidly+became+Hinduism&source=bl&ots=Ph783Gc-j3b&sig=UQkOqmjzJaCX8IaJ8ksLB1vhAT0&hl=en&sa=X&ei=ozS0U_irMY_JuAS2qoCgBw&ved=0CBsQ6AewAA#v=onepage&q=The%20foreigners%2C%20like%20their%20forerunners%20the%20Sakas%20and%20the%20Yueh-chi%2C%20universally%20yielded%20to%20the%20wonderful%20assimilative%20powers%20of%20Hinduism%2C%20and%20rapidly%20became%20Hinduism&f=false, accessed on
2. Flow of History
3. Shashi Tharoor, 'Who is an Indian? A Nation of Minorities,' 5th annual lecture, National Commission of Minorities, athttp://www.rediff.com/news/slide-show/slide-show-1-we-are-all-mi-norities-in-india-says-shashi-tharoor/20120907.htm#1
4. Angus Maddison, *The World Economy: A Millennial Perspective*, OECD Development Centre, June 12, 2001.
5. http://www.intellihub.com/gandhis-vision-of-a-stateless-society/
6. http://samvada.org/2012/news/glorious-87-rashtriya-swayamsevak-sangh-rss-turns-87-on-today-on-vijayadashami/
7. Transporter Movie (20th Century Fox and Europa Corp. Distribution), Directors Louis Leterrier and Corey Yuen, Produced by Luc Besson and Stephen Chas- man
8. http://www.tatasteel100.com/heritage/history/history06.asp

9. A.P.J. Abdul Kalam, Srijan Pal Singh, Target 3 Billion, Magarapatta website (Penguin India)
10. Chandrahas Choudhary, "MBA Culture Crushes Caste in India," Bloomberg Businessweek, http://www.bloombergview.com/articles/2014-07-20/mba-culture- crushes-caste-in-india
11. http://timesofindia.indiatimes.com/home/opinion/edit-page/The-nowhere-to-go-crowd/articleshow/15535891.cms
12. John Restakis, *Humanizing the Economy, Cooperatives in the Age of Capital* (New Society Publishers, 2010), p. 16.
13. Remittance Needs and Opportunities in India (GIZ-NABARD) *MSME Mentor
14. http://www.dailymail.co.uk/news/article-2088297/BBC-refuses-apologise-tasteless-Top-Gear-India-special.html
15. Aavin http://www.aavinmilk.com/organisation.html
16. http://www.amul.com/m/organisation
17. http://www.indiancooperative.com/tag/comfed/
18. http://www.sarasmilkfed.rajasthan.gov.in/Tender/EOI%20D.CONS.070714.Pdf
19. http://articles.economictimes.indiatimes.com/2010-09-21/news/27572770_1_procurement-price-lakh-litre-milk-powder-and-butter
20. Brenden Greeley, "Germany's Merkel Avoids Painful Economic Reforms," Bloomberg *Businessweek*, http://www.businessweek.com/articles/2014-07-17/ germanys-merkel-avoids-painful-economic-reforms
21. "The Gujarat Model" (Cover Story), *India Today Group*, April 14, 2014.
22. http://www.hindustantimes.com/elections2014/state-of-the-states/sops-will-continue-bjp-to-link-them-to-asset-creation-jaitley/article1-1202754.aspx (*Hindustan Times*, Jaitley's Asset Creation Opinion)
23. http://aajeevika.gov.in/ (Aajeevika, NRLM)

Books

Chapter 1

- Peter A. Clayton and John Dent, *The Ancient River Civilizations: Western Man and the Modern World* (Elsevier, 1973)
- *Discovery of India:* Jawahar Lal Nehru
- Axel Michaels, *Hinduism: Past and Present*, trans. Barbara Harshav (Princeton University Press, 2003)
- *History of Religions:* BK Smith
- *The Early History of India:* Vincent A. Smith
- *A Rough Guide to Kushan History:* Robert Bracey
- William Woodthorpe Tarn, *The Greeks in Bactria and India*, first edition (Cambridge University Press, 2010)
- Michael Tobias, *Life Force: The World of Jainis* (Jain Publishing House)
- *The Flow of History, A Dynamic and Graphical Approach to Teaching History:* Chris Butler

- *An Introduction to Buddhism: Teachings, History and Practices:* Peter Harvey
- Angus Maddison, *The World Economy: A Millennial Perspective*, OECD Development Centre, June 12, 2001.
- Envisioning India

Chapter 2

- Richard H.K. Vietor, *How Countries Compete: Strategy, Structure and Government in the Global Economy* (Harvard Business Review, 2007)
- Arvind Kejriwal, *Swaraj* (Harper Collins, 2014)
- A.P.J. Abdul Kalam, Srijan Pal Singh, *Target 3 Billion* (Penguin India, 2011)
- Elinor Ostrom, *Governing the Commons: The Evolution of Institutions for Collective Action*, (Cambridge University Press,1990).
- John Restakis, *Humanizing the Economy, Cooperatives in the Age of Capital* (New Society Publishers, 2010), p. 16.

Index